This cookbook belongs to:

LEISURE ARTS, INC.
LITTLE ROCK, ARKANSAS

THE COOKIE JAR

I do respect the iron man who, when he's faced with cookies, can
Confine himself to one or two and leave the rest for me and you!
— FROM AN ANTIQUE COOKBOOK

EDITORIAL STAFF

Editor-in-Chief: Anne Van Wagner Childs
Executive Director: Sandra Graham Case
Executive Editor: Susan Frantz Wiles
Publications Director: Carla Bentley
Creative Art Director: Gloria Bearden
Production Art Director: Melinda Stout

FOODS
Foods Editor: Celia Fahr Harkey, R.D.
Assistant Foods Editor: Jane Kenner Prather
Test Kitchen Assistants: Nora Faye Spencer Clift and
　　Leslie Belote Dunn

ART
Book/Magazine Art Director: Diane M. Ghegan
Senior Production Artist: Michael A. Spigner
Photography Stylist: Karen Smart Hall

DESIGN
Design Director: Patricia Wallenfang Sowers

EDITORIAL
Associate Editor: Linda L. Trimble
Senior Editorial Writer: Tammi Williamson Bradley
Editorial Writers: Darla Burdette Kelsay and
　　Robyn Sheffield-Edwards
Editorial Associate: Terri Leming Davidson
Copy Editor: Laura Lee Weland

ADVERTISING AND DIRECT MAIL
Senior Editor: Tena Kelley Vaughn
Copywriters: Steven M. Cooper, Marla Shivers,
　　and Jonathon Walker
Designer: Rhonda H. Hestir
Art Director: Jeff Curtis
Production Artist: Linda Lovette Smart

BUSINESS STAFF

Publisher: Bruce Akin
Controller: Tom Siebenmorgen
Retail Sales Director: Richard Tignor
Retail Marketing Director: Pam Stebbins
Retail Customer Services Director: Margaret Sweetin
Marketing Manager: Russ Barnett

Executive Director of Marketing and Circulation:
　　Guy A. Crossley
Circulation Manager: Byron L. Taylor
Print Production Manager: Laura Lockhart
Print Production Coordinator: Nancy Reddick Lister

THE COOKIE JAR

*E*veryone loves fresh-baked cookies, and this irresistible recipe book is brimming with a delicious assortment of ooey, gooey, crispy, crunchy confections. A must for beginning cooks and experienced bakers alike, it includes thirteen exciting collections of cookies. You'll find traditional favorites, as well as kid-pleasing goodies that children can help make and decorate. Adults will savor our selections for sophisticated tastes, and there are scrumptious tidbits for gift-giving and parties, too. There are also delightful surprises from around the world and cookies to welcome each season and celebrate special days. Straight from Santa's bakeshop, our Christmas collection will sweeten the holidays! Keeping in mind today's emphasis on healthier eating, we even developed a section of lower-fat cookies that are not only good, but they're practically guilt-free! Now there's no need to search through your recipe files and piles of cookbooks when your sweet tooth needs satisfying — just reach for The Cookie Jar *and pull out the perfect treat!*

Anne Childs

Table of Contents

Table of Contents

Table of Contents

SPECIAL OCCASIONS 68

SOPHISTICATED TASTES 76

AROUND THE WORLD 84

Table of Contents

WINTER WARMERS

The joys of wintertime baking extend far beyond the holiday season. As the first powdery snow blankets the earth, the comforting aromas and tastes of home-baked cookies are delicious winter warmers. In this collection of sweet confections, you'll find cookies that reflect the appeal of a new-fallen snow and celebrate favorite winter occasions, plus an assortment of chunky, nutty treats to make any day more special. Come in from the cold to these delectable sweets!

Raspberry Chocolate Chip Cookies	Poppy Seed Cookies
Hazelnut Macaroons	Rugelach
Nutty Peanut Butter Brownies	New Year's Toast Cookies
Cinnamon-Brown Sugar Snowflakes	Sweetheart Cookies
Snowy Day Cookies	Chocolate-Peanut Butter Cookies

(Previous page) A mug of cocoa and these tempting sweets will chase the chill from a wintry day! Topped with lots of crunchy peanuts, Nutty Peanut Butter Brownies (clockwise from left) are moist and chewy. Ground hazelnuts make Hazelnut Macaroons unforgettable melt-in-your-mouth treats. Crispy Cinnamon-Brown Sugar Snowflakes are decorated with frosty icing patterns. Rich macadamia nuts and a drizzling of fruity icing bring a pleasing flavor combination to soft Raspberry Chocolate Chip Cookies.

RASPBERRY CHOCOLATE CHIP COOKIES

COOKIES
- 2 packages (10 ounces each) raspberry-flavored semisweet chocolate chips, divided
- 3/4 cup butter or margarine, softened
- 1/2 cup granulated sugar
- 1/2 cup firmly packed brown sugar
- 2 eggs
- 1 teaspoon vanilla extract
- 2 1/2 cups all-purpose flour
- 3/4 teaspoon baking soda
- 3/4 teaspoon baking powder
- 1/2 teaspoon salt
- 1 cup coarsely chopped macadamia nuts

ICING
- 1 cup sifted confectioners sugar
- 3 tablespoons raspberry-flavored liqueur
  Burgundy paste food coloring

Preheat oven to 375 degrees. For cookies, place 1 package of chocolate chips in a small microwave-safe bowl. Microwave on medium-high power (80%) 1 minute; stir. Microwave 1 minute longer; stir until melted. In a large bowl, cream butter and sugars until fluffy. Add eggs and vanilla; beat until smooth. Stir in melted chocolate. In a medium bowl, combine flour, baking soda, baking powder, and salt. Add dry ingredients to creamed mixture; stir until a soft dough forms. Stir in remaining package of chocolate chips and macadamia nuts. Drop tablespoonfuls of dough 2 inches apart onto an ungreased baking sheet. Bake 7 to 9 minutes or until bottoms are lightly browned. Transfer cookies to a wire rack with waxed paper underneath to cool.

For icing, combine confectioners sugar and liqueur in a small bowl; stir until smooth. Tint burgundy. Spoon icing into a pastry bag fitted with a small round tip. Pipe icing onto cookies. Allow icing to harden. Store in an airtight container.

Yield: about 7 dozen cookies

HAZELNUT MACAROONS

- 3 egg whites
- 1/2 teaspoon vanilla extract
- 1/2 teaspoon cream of tartar
- 1 cup sugar
- 1 2/3 cups finely ground hazelnuts

Preheat oven to 300 degrees. In a medium bowl, beat egg whites until soft peaks form. Add vanilla and cream of tartar. Gradually add sugar, beating until mixture is very stiff. Gently fold hazelnuts into egg white mixture. Drop teaspoonfuls of mixture 2 inches apart onto a baking sheet lined with parchment paper. Bake 17 to 20 minutes or until edges are lightly browned. Transfer cookies to a wire rack to cool. Store in an airtight container.

Yield: about 5 1/2 dozen cookies

NUTTY PEANUT BUTTER BROWNIES

- 3/4 cup smooth peanut butter
- 1/2 cup butter or margarine, softened
- 1 1/2 cups firmly packed brown sugar
- 2 eggs
- 2 teaspoons vanilla extract
- 1 1/2 cups all-purpose flour
- 1 1/2 teaspoons baking powder
- 1/8 teaspoon salt
- 1/2 cup chopped peanuts

Preheat oven to 375 degrees. In a large bowl, cream peanut butter, butter, and brown sugar until fluffy. Add eggs and vanilla; beat until smooth. In a small bowl, combine flour, baking powder, and salt. Add dry ingredients to creamed mixture; stir until well blended. Line a 9 x 13-inch baking pan with aluminum foil, extending foil over ends of pan; grease foil. Spread batter in prepared pan; sprinkle peanuts over top. Bake 15 to 18 minutes or until edges are lightly browned. Cool in pan 10 minutes. Use ends of foil to lift brownie from pan. Cut warm brownies into 2-inch squares; cool completely. Store in an airtight container.

Yield: about 2 dozen brownies

CINNAMON-BROWN SUGAR SNOWFLAKES

- 3/4 cup butter or margarine, softened
- 1 1/4 cups firmly packed brown sugar
- 1 egg
- 1 teaspoon vanilla extract
- 1 3/4 cups all-purpose flour
- 1 1/2 teaspoons ground cinnamon, divided
- 1 teaspoon baking powder
- 2 tablespoons granulated sugar
  Purchased white decorating icing to decorate

Preheat oven to 375 degrees. In a large bowl, cream butter and brown sugar until fluffy. Add egg and vanilla; beat until smooth. In a small bowl, combine flour, 1 teaspoon cinnamon, and baking powder. Stir dry ingredients into creamed mixture. Drop teaspoonfuls of dough 3 inches apart onto an ungreased baking sheet. In a small bowl, combine granulated sugar and remaining cinnamon. Flatten cookies with a glass dipped in sugar mixture. Bake 4 to 5 minutes or until edges are very lightly browned. Transfer cookies to a wire rack to cool. Use icing to pipe desired snowflake designs onto cookies. Allow icing to harden. Store in an airtight container.

Yield: about 8 dozen cookies

SNOWY DAY COOKIES

  1 cup butter or margarine, softened
  2 cups sifted confectioners sugar,
       divided
  1 teaspoon almond extract
  1/2 teaspoon vanilla extract
  2 1/4 cups all-purpose flour
  1/4 teaspoon salt
  1 cup slivered almonds, toasted and
       coarsely ground

Preheat oven to 350 degrees. In a large bowl, cream butter and 1/2 cup confectioners sugar until fluffy. Stir in extracts. In a medium bowl, combine flour and salt. Add dry ingredients to creamed mixture; stir until a soft dough forms. Stir in almonds. Shape dough into 1-inch balls and place 2 inches apart on an ungreased baking sheet. Bake 15 to 20 minutes or until bottoms are lightly browned. Roll warm cookies in remaining 1 1/2 cups confectioners sugar. Transfer cookies to waxed paper; cool completely. Roll in confectioners sugar again. Store in an airtight container.

Yield: about 4 1/2 dozen cookies

Rolled in confectioners sugar to resemble tiny snowballs, Snowy Day Cookies are yummy almond-flavored bites. You can warm up your serving basket with a simple square of flannel that's edged with running stitches, or for a tasty gift, present some of the cookies in a jar topped with a padded fabric lid.

Shaped like the Star of David, Poppy Seed Cookies have a light lemony flavor and crunchy texture. Crescent-shaped Rugelach, traditional Hanukkah pastries, present a filling of raisins and walnuts rolled in a flaky cream cheese crust.

POPPY SEED COOKIES

3/4 cup vegetable oil
1 cup sugar
3 eggs
2 teaspoons vanilla extract
1 teaspoon lemon extract
3 1/2 cups all-purpose flour
1/4 cup poppy seed
1 teaspoon baking powder
1/8 teaspoon salt

Preheat oven to 400 degrees. In a large bowl, beat oil and sugar until well blended. Add eggs and extracts; beat until smooth. In a medium bowl, combine flour, poppy seed, baking powder, and salt. Add dry ingredients to sugar mixture; stir until a soft dough forms. Divide dough into fourths. On a heavily floured surface, use a floured rolling pin to roll out one fourth of dough to 1/4-inch thickness. Use a floured 3-inch Star of David-shaped cookie cutter to cut out cookies. Using a spatula, transfer to a greased baking sheet. Bake 5 to 7 minutes or until edges are lightly browned. Transfer cookies to a wire rack to cool. Repeat with remaining dough. Store in an airtight container.

Yield: about 4 1/2 dozen cookies

RUGELACH

DOUGH

1 package (8 ounces) cream cheese, softened
3/4 cup butter or margarine, softened
2 tablespoons sugar
1 teaspoon vanilla extract
1 1/2 cups all-purpose flour

FILLING

3/4 cup raisins
1/4 cup granulated sugar
1/4 cup firmly packed brown sugar
1 1/2 teaspoons ground cinnamon
1 cup coarsely chopped toasted walnuts
3 tablespoons butter or margarine, softened and divided

For dough, beat cream cheese, butter, sugar, and vanilla in a medium bowl until fluffy. Add flour; stir until a soft dough forms. Divide dough into 3 balls. Wrap in plastic wrap and chill overnight.

For filling, combine raisins, sugars, and cinnamon in a food processor; process until raisins are coarsely chopped. Add walnuts and continue to process until walnuts are finely chopped.

Preheat oven to 350 degrees. On a heavily floured surface, use a floured rolling pin to roll 1 ball of dough into a 12-inch circle. Spread 1 tablespoon butter over dough circle. Sprinkle about 9 tablespoons filling over buttered dough; press lightly into dough. Using a pizza cutter, cut dough into quarters; cut each quarter into 3 wedges. Beginning at wide end, roll up each wedge. Transfer to a baking sheet lined with parchment paper. Bake 15 to 20 minutes or until edges are lightly browned. Transfer cookies to a wire rack to cool. Repeat with remaining dough and filling. Store in an airtight container.

Yield: 3 dozen cookies

Gaily decorated with colored icing and dragées, these party horn- and mask-shaped New Year's Toast Cookies will help you ring in the holiday with delicious style. The cutout cookies are laced with white wine for added spirit and served in a paper party hat. A simple tag tied with a shiny ribbon bow conveys a holiday greeting to your guests.

NEW YEAR'S TOAST COOKIES

COOKIES

1 1/2 cups butter or margarine, softened
2 cups sugar
1/2 cup white wine
4 egg yolks
2 egg whites
6 cups all-purpose flour

ICING

6 cups sifted confectioners sugar
8 to 10 tablespoons milk
1/2 teaspoon vanilla extract
Purple, green, blue, and pink paste food coloring
6-inch wooden skewers (for masks) and dragées to decorate

Note: Use patterns, page 116, and follow Cutting Out Cookies, page 122.

For cookies, cream butter and sugar in a large bowl until fluffy. Add wine and egg yolks; beat until smooth. In a small bowl, beat egg whites until soft peaks form. Fold egg whites into creamed mixture. Add flour to creamed mixture, gently stirring until a soft dough forms. Divide dough into fourths. Wrap in plastic wrap and chill 2 hours.

Preheat oven to 375 degrees. On a lightly floured surface, use a floured rolling pin to roll out one fourth of dough to 1/8-inch thickness. Cut out cookies. Transfer to a lightly greased baking sheet. Insert a wooden skewer into 1 side of each mask

cookie. Bake 8 to 10 minutes or until bottoms are lightly browned. Transfer cookies to a wire rack with waxed paper underneath to cool. Repeat with remaining dough.

For icing, combine confectioners sugar, 8 tablespoons milk, and vanilla in a medium bowl; stir until smooth. Add additional milk, 1/2 teaspoon at a time, for desired consistency. Divide icing into 4 small bowls. Tint purple, green, blue, and pink. Ice cookies, adding dots and swirls of a second color of icing or sprinkling with dragées if desired. Allow icing to harden. Store in an airtight container.

Yield: about 10 dozen cookies

13

SWEETHEART COOKIES

COOKIES

- 1/2 cup butter or margarine, softened
- 1/2 cup firmly packed brown sugar
- 3/4 cup honey
- 1 egg
- 1 teaspoon lemon extract
- 3 cups all-purpose flour
- 3/4 teaspoon baking soda
- 1/2 teaspoon ground cinnamon
- 1/4 teaspoon salt

ICING

- 3 cups sifted confectioners sugar
- 1/3 cup vegetable shortening
- 1/3 cup butter or margarine, softened
- 3/4 teaspoon lemon extract
- 2 tablespoons milk
  Green and pink paste food
  coloring

For cookies, cream butter and brown sugar until fluffy. Add honey, egg, and lemon extract; beat until smooth. In a medium bowl, combine flour, baking soda, cinnamon, and salt. Gradually add dry ingredients to creamed mixture; stir until a soft dough forms. Divide dough in half. Wrap in plastic wrap and chill 4 hours.

Preheat oven to 350 degrees. On a lightly floured surface, use a floured rolling pin to roll out half of dough to 1/4-inch thickness. Use a variety of heart-shaped cookie cutters to cut out cookies and centers of some cookies. Transfer to a greased baking sheet. Bake 7 to 10 minutes or until cookies are firm to the touch. Cool cookies on pan 2 minutes; transfer to a wire rack with waxed paper underneath to cool completely. Repeat with remaining dough.

For icing, combine confectioners sugar, shortening, butter, lemon extract, and milk in a medium bowl; beat until smooth. Place 1/3 cup icing in a small bowl; tint green. Tint remaining icing pink. Spoon icing into pastry bags. Using a variety of decorating

Touched with honey, Sweetheart Cookies let you say "Be My Valentine!" in a delectable way. The soft, spicy cookies are cut in heart shapes and beautifully decorated with lemony icing.

, pipe desired decorations onto cookies.
ow icing to harden. Store cookies in a
gle layer in an airtight container.

ld: about 4 dozen 1¼- to 3¼-inch
kies

HOCOLATE-PEANUT
TTER COOKIES

¹⁄₂ cup butter or margarine, softened
¹⁄₂ cup smooth peanut butter
1 cup sifted confectioners sugar
¹⁄₄ cup firmly packed brown sugar
1 egg
1 teaspoon vanilla extract
1 cup all-purpose flour
¹⁄₂ cup cocoa
¹⁄₄ teaspoon salt

e: Use patterns, page 116, and follow
ting Out Cookies, page 122, or use
rchased 2³⁄₄ x 4-inch cookie cutters.
n a large bowl, cream butter, peanut
ter, and sugars until fluffy. Add egg and
illa; beat until smooth. In a small bowl,
mbine flour, cocoa, and salt. Add dry
redients to creamed mixture; stir until a
t dough forms. Cover dough and chill
ours.
Preheat oven to 375 degrees. On a lightly
ured surface, use a floured rolling pin to
out dough to ¹⁄₈-inch thickness. Cut out
kies. Place 2 inches apart on a greased
king sheet. Bake 5 to 7 minutes or until
es are firm. Transfer cookies to a wire
k to cool. Store in an airtight container.

ld: about 2¹⁄₂ dozen cookies

Celebrate Presidents' Day with these familiar faces and flavors! Cut in the shapes of Abraham Lincoln and George Washington, Chocolate-Peanut Butter Cookies are soft and chewy treats. For sharing, pack the cookies in one of these papier-mâché carriers embellished with fused-on fabrics or patriotic ribbon. We used our cookie cutter as a pattern for the Lincoln fabric silhouette.

SPRING SENSATIONS

As spring blooms to life, awaken your cookie jar with these scrumptious sweets. Our tasty assortment mirrors the season's freshness with pretty flowers, colorful carrots, tiny nests, and even candy-tailed Easter bunnies! To celebrate other special spring days, we include airy macaroons for Passover, nutty Saint Patrick's Day cookies, and a red-hot selection for April Fools' Day. You'll enjoy greeting spring and springtime guests with these delightful treats!

Daffodil Cookies	Blarney Stones
Orange-Nut Shortbread	April Fools' Cookies
Oatmeal-Fruit Cookies	Springtime Bunnies
Easter Egg Nests	Carrot Cookies
Afternoon Tea Cakes	Cinnamon-Almond Macaroons
Strawberry Pie Crust Cookies	Spring Baskets

(Previous page) *Oatmeal-Fruit Cookies* (from left) *are studded with dried apricots and dates, and Easter Egg Nests are chocolaty coconut treats filled with gourmet jelly beans! Baked to resemble little flowers, Daffodil Cookies are rich cream cheese pastries with a pineapple filling. Orange-Nut Shortbread is flavored with ground pecans and freshly grated orange zest.*

DAFFODIL COOKIES

- 3/4 cup butter or margarine, softened
- 4 1/2 ounces cream cheese, softened
- 1 3/4 cups all-purpose flour
- 1/4 cup cornstarch
   Green and yellow paste food coloring
- 1 egg
- 2 teaspoons water
- 1/2 cup pineapple preserves

In a medium bowl, cream butter and cream cheese until well blended. In a small bowl, combine flour and cornstarch. Add dry ingredients to creamed mixture; stir until a soft dough forms. Tint 1/3 cup of dough green and remaining dough yellow. Divide yellow dough into thirds. Wrap green and yellow dough in plastic wrap and chill 1 hour.

Preheat oven to 375 degrees. On a lightly floured surface, use a floured rolling pin to roll out one third of yellow dough to 1/8-inch thickness. In a small bowl, whisk egg and water until well blended. Use a 3-inch-diameter fluted-edge cookie cutter to cut out cookies. Transfer to an ungreased baking sheet. Overlap 2 edges to form cone-shaped cookies, brushing overlapped edges with egg mixture to seal. Roll out green dough to 1/16-inch thickness. Cut 1/4 x 3-inch strips for leaves. Brush bottom edges of cookies with egg mixture. Fold strips in half and place 1 on each cookie (Fig. 1).

Fig. 1

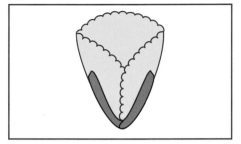

Place about 1/2 teaspoon pineapple preserves on top portion of each cookie. Bake 12 to 15 minutes or until edges are lightly browned. Transfer cookies to a wire rack to cool. Repeat with remaining dough and preserves. Store in an airtight container.

Yield: about 3 dozen cookies

ORANGE-NUT SHORTBREAD

- 3/4 cup butter or margarine, softened
- 1/2 cup sugar
- 2 teaspoons grated orange zest
- 1/2 teaspoon orange extract
- 1 cup all-purpose flour
- 1/2 cup cornstarch
- 1/2 cup coarsely ground pecans

Preheat oven to 350 degrees. In a medium bowl, cream butter, sugar, orange zest, and orange extract until fluffy. In a small bowl, combine flour and cornstarch. Add dry ingredients to creamed mixture; stir until a soft dough forms. Stir in pecans. Line a 9-inch square baking pan with aluminum foil, extending foil over opposite sides; grease foil. Press dough into bottom of prepared pan. Bake 45 to 50 minutes or until golden in color. Use ends of foil to immediately lift shortbread from pan. Cut warm shortbread into 1 1/2 x 2-inch bars; cool completely. Store in an airtight container.

Yield: about 2 dozen bars

OATMEAL-FRUIT COOKIES

- 1/2 cup butter or margarine, softened
- 3/4 cup firmly packed brown sugar
- 1 egg
- 2 tablespoons milk
- 1 teaspoon vanilla extract
- 1/2 teaspoon almond extract
- 2/3 cup all-purpose flour
- 1/2 teaspoon baking soda
- 1/2 teaspoon salt
- 1 1/2 cups old-fashioned oats
- 1/2 cup chopped dried apricots
- 1/2 cup chopped dates
- 1/2 cup sliced almonds, toasted
   Granulated sugar

Preheat oven to 350 degrees. In a large bowl, cream butter and brown sugar until fluffy. Add egg, milk, and extracts; beat un smooth. In a small bowl, combine flour, baking soda, and salt. Add dry ingredients to creamed mixture; stir until a soft dough forms. Stir in oats, apricots, dates, and almonds. Drop tablespoonfuls of dough 3 inches apart onto a baking sheet lined with parchment paper. Flatten cookies wit bottom of a glass dipped in granulated sugar. Bake 8 to 10 minutes or until edges are lightly browned. Cool cookies on pan 3 minutes; transfer to a wire rack to cool completely. Store in an airtight container.

Yield: about 3 1/2 dozen cookies

EASTER EGG NESTS

- 1/2 cup plus 2 tablespoons sweetened condensed milk (1/2 of a 14-ounce can)
- 1/4 cup semisweet chocolate chips
- 2 cups sweetened finely shredded coconut
- 1/2 cup finely chopped pecans
- 1/2 cup graham cracker crumbs
- 4 ounces gourmet jelly beans

Sharing these soft, chewy Afternoon Tea Cakes and a refreshing pot of tea with good friends is a delicious way to [en]bance a lively conversation. Touched with a hint of orange, the cakes are simply dreamy! A floral box keeps them [fre]sh until teatime.

[C]ombine sweetened condensed milk and [cho]colate chips in a heavy small saucepan [ove]r medium heat. Stirring frequently, heat [unt]il chocolate chips are melted. Reduce [hea]t to low. Add coconut, pecans, and [cra]cker crumbs; stir until well blended. [Re]move from heat. Drop teaspoonfuls of [coo]kie mixture 1 inch apart onto a greased [ba]king sheet. Press 3 jelly beans into center [of e]ach cookie. Chill on pan to allow [cho]colate to harden. Store in an airtight [con]tainer in a cool place.

[Yie]ld: about 3¹/₂ dozen cookies

AFTERNOON TEA CAKES

¹/₂ cup butter or margarine, softened
1 cup sugar
1 egg
1 teaspoon vanilla extract
¹/₄ teaspoon orange extract
2 cups all-purpose flour
2 teaspoons baking powder
¹/₂ teaspoon salt

In a medium bowl, cream butter and sugar until fluffy. Add egg and extracts; beat until smooth. In a small bowl, combine flour, baking powder, and salt. Add dry ingredients to creamed mixture; stir until a

soft dough forms. Divide dough into fourths. Wrap in plastic wrap and chill 1 to 2 hours.

Preheat oven to 400 degrees. On a lightly floured surface, use a floured rolling pin to roll out one fourth of dough to ¹/₈-inch thickness. Use a 2¹/₂-inch-diameter fluted-edge cookie cutter to cut out cookies. Place 2 inches apart on a lightly greased baking sheet. Bake 6 to 8 minutes or until edges are lightly browned. Transfer cookies to a wire rack to cool. Repeat with remaining dough. Store in an airtight container.

Yield: about 3¹/₂ dozen cookies

STRAWBERRY PIE CRUST COOKIES

    3 tablespoons strawberry-flavored
        gelatin, divided
    2 tablespoons granulated sugar
    2 crusts from a 15-ounce package of
        refrigerated pie crusts, at room
        temperature
    1 egg white
    1 teaspoon water
      Red and green decorating sugar

Note: Use pattern, page 117, and follow Cutting Out Cookies, page 122, or use a purchased 2 x 2³/₄-inch cookie cutter.

Preheat oven to 425 degrees. In a small bowl, combine 2 tablespoons gelatin and granulated sugar. Unfold first crust on a lightly floured surface; press creases flat. In a small bowl, whisk egg white and water. Brush a small amount of egg white mixture over crust. Sprinkle gelatin mixture over crust. Unfold second crust on a lightly floured surface; press creases flat. Brush a small amount of egg white mixture over second crust. Place egg white side down on first crust; gently press together. Cut out cookies. Transfer to a lightly greased baking sheet; brush with egg white mixture. Covering tops of cookies with a piece of paper, sprinkle remaining 1 tablespoon gelatin over cookies; repeat with red decorating sugar. Covering red areas with paper, sprinkle tops of cookies with green decorating sugar. Bake 9 to 11 minutes or until bottoms are lightly browned. Transfer cookies to a wire rack to cool. Store in an airtight container.

Yield: about 2 dozen cookies

If you're really lucky on Saint Patrick's Day, you'll discover a pot of Blarney Stones at the end of the rainbow. Loaded with peanuts and raisins, the soft, spicy nuggets are worth their weight in gold!

BLARNEY STONES

    ³/₄ cup butter or margarine, softened
    1 cup sugar
    2 eggs
    1¹/₂ teaspoons vanilla extract
    1³/₄ cups all-purpose flour
    1 teaspoon ground allspice
    ¹/₂ teaspoon baking soda
    1 can (12 ounces) salted peanuts
    1 cup golden raisins

Preheat oven to 375 degrees. In a large bowl, cream butter and sugar until fluffy. Add eggs and vanilla; beat until smooth. I small bowl, combine flour, allspice, and baking soda. Add dry ingredients to

So pretty and so incredibly easy to make, Strawberry Pie Crust Cookies get their delicate taste from a sprinkling of strawberry-flavored gelatin. Red and green decorating sugar provides their vibrant color. As a special treat for your family, pack the cookies in a purchased berry basket.

amed mixture; stir until a soft dough
ms. Stir in peanuts and raisins. Drop
lespoonfuls of dough 2 inches apart onto
reased baking sheet. Bake 9 to
minutes or until edges are lightly
wned. Transfer cookies to a wire rack to
ol. Store in an airtight container.

ld: about 4¹/₂ dozen cookies

RIL FOOLS' COOKIES

OKIES

/₂ cup small red cinnamon candies
/₂ cup sugar
/₂ cups all-purpose flour
/₂ cup butter or margarine, softened
 1 egg
 1 teaspoon baking powder
/₈ teaspoon cinnamon-flavored oil
      (used in candy making)

NG

/₂ cups sifted confectioners sugar
 5 tablespoons plus 1 teaspoon milk
      Red paste food coloring

For cookies, combine candies and sugar
a food processor; pulse process several
es until candies are finely chopped. Add
naining ingredients to food processor;
cess 1 minute or until mixture is well
nded. Shape dough into two 8-inch-long
ls. Wrap in plastic wrap and chill 2 hours
until firm.

Preheat oven to 375 degrees. Cut dough
o ¹/₄-inch slices. Place 2 inches apart on
aking sheet lined with parchment paper.
ke 6 to 8 minutes or until edges are
tly browned. Cool cookies on pan
ninutes; transfer to a wire rack with
xed paper underneath to cool
mpletely.

For icing, combine confectioners sugar
d milk; beat until smooth. Tint red. Ice
okies. Allow icing to harden. Store in an
tight container.

ld: about 4 dozen cookies

It's no joke — our April Fools' Cookies are delightfully different! While they look like cherry-studded treats, the iced cookies are really flavored with cinnamon oil and candies for a taste that's red hot.

Preheat oven to 350 degrees. On a lightly floured surface, use a floured rolling pin to roll out half of dough to slightly less than 1/4-inch thickness. Cut out cookies. Place 2 inches apart on a lightly greased baking sheet. Press jelly beans into cookies for ears and tails. Bake 8 to 10 minutes or until bottoms are lightly browned. Transfer cookies to a wire rack to cool. Repeat with remaining dough and jelly beans. Store in an airtight container.

Yield: about 2 dozen cookies

CARROT COOKIES

COOKIES
- 1 cup butter or margarine, softened
- 1 cup sugar
- 2 eggs
- 2 teaspoons vanilla extract
  Orange paste food coloring
- 3 medium carrots, quartered
- 1/2 cup chopped pecans
- 1/2 cup golden raisins
- 1 3/4 cups all-purpose flour
- 1/4 cup cornstarch
- 1 teaspoon baking powder
- 1 teaspoon ground cinnamon
- 3/4 teaspoon ground allspice
- 1/4 teaspoon salt

GLAZE
- 1 1/2 cups sifted confectioners sugar
- 2 tablespoons plus 1 teaspoon milk
  Orange paste food coloring

BUTTERCREAM ICING
- 1 1/2 cups sifted confectioners sugar
- 3 tablespoons vegetable shortening
- 3 tablespoons butter or margarine, softened
- 1 1/2 tablespoons milk
- 1/2 teaspoon vanilla extract
  Green paste food coloring

Accented with jelly bean tails and ears, lightly sweet Springtime Bunnies will help you spread "hoppy" Easter wishes. For a pretty centerpiece, display a few of your cookies in a basket of Easter grass.

SPRINGTIME BUNNIES

- 3/4 cup butter or margarine, softened
- 1/2 cup granulated sugar
- 1/2 cup sifted confectioners sugar
- 1 egg
- 1 1/2 teaspoons vanilla extract
- 2 1/4 cups all-purpose flour
- 1/2 teaspoon baking soda
- 1/2 teaspoon cream of tartar
- 3 1/2 ounces gourmet jelly beans

Note: Use pattern, page 117, and follow Cutting Out Cookies, page 122, or use a purchased 4 x 3 1/4-inch cookie cutter.

In a large bowl, cream butter and sugars until fluffy. Add egg and vanilla; beat until smooth. In a medium bowl, combine flour, baking soda, and cream of tartar. Add dry ingredients to creamed mixture; stir until a soft dough forms. Divide dough in half. Wrap in plastic wrap and chill 2 hours.

Seasoned cooks will delight in baking a batch of cake-like Carrot Cookies for the Easter bunny (and other holiday visitors). Decorated with a sweet glaze and buttercream icing, the spicy cookies are filled with golden raisins, chopped pecans, and fresh carrots.

te: Use pattern, page 117, and follow tting Out Cookies, page 122, or use a rchased 1³/₄ x 4³/₄-inch cookie cutter.

For cookies, cream butter and sugar in a ge bowl until fluffy. Add eggs and vanilla; at until smooth. Tint orange. Place rrots, pecans, and raisins in a food ocessor; process until finely chopped. In small bowl, combine flour, cornstarch, king powder, cinnamon, allspice, and lt. Add carrot mixture and dry ingredients creamed mixture; stir until a soft dough rms. Divide dough into fourths. Wrap in astic wrap and chill 3 hours or until firm.

Preheat oven to 375 degrees. On a heavily floured surface, use a floured rolling pin to roll out one fourth of dough to ¹/₄-inch thickness. Cut out cookies. Transfer to an ungreased baking sheet. Bake 7 to 9 minutes or until edges are lightly browned. Transfer cookies to a wire rack with waxed paper underneath to cool. Repeat with remaining dough.

For glaze, combine confectioners sugar and milk in a small bowl; beat until smooth. Tint orange. Spoon glaze onto large ends of carrot cookies. Allow glaze to harden.

For buttercream icing, combine confectioners sugar, shortening, butter, milk, and vanilla in a small bowl; beat until smooth. Tint green. Spoon icing into a pastry bag fitted with a grass tip. Pipe icing onto tops of cookies to resemble leaves. Allow icing to harden. Store in single layers between sheets of waxed paper in an airtight container.

Yield: about 3¹/₂ dozen cookies

SPRING BASKETS

COOKIES
- ¹/₂ cup butter or margarine, softened
- ³/₄ cup plus 2 tablespoons sugar
- ¹/₂ cup sour cream
- 1 egg
- 1 teaspoon almond extract
- 2¹/₄ cups all-purpose flour
- ¹/₂ cup slivered almonds, toasted and finely ground
- 1 teaspoon baking powder
- ¹/₂ teaspoon baking soda
- ¹/₄ teaspoon salt

ICING
- 6 cups sifted confectioners sugar
- ³/₄ cup vegetable shortening
- ³/₄ cup butter or margarine, softened
- 1¹/₂ teaspoons almond extract
- 3 to 4 tablespoons milk
  Yellow, blue, pink, green, and tan pastel paste food coloring

Note: Use pattern, page 117, and follow Cutting Out Cookies, page 122.

For cookies, cream butter and sugar in large bowl until fluffy. Add sour cream, egg, and almond extract; beat until smooth. In medium bowl, combine flour, almonds, baking powder, baking soda, and salt. Add dry ingredients to creamed mixture; stir until a soft dough forms. Divide dough into thirds. Wrap in plastic wrap and chill overnight.

Preheat oven to 350 degrees. On a lightly floured surface, use a floured rolling pin to roll out one third of dough to ¹/₄-inch thickness. Cut out cookies. Place 2 inches apart on a greased baking sheet. Bake 8 to 10 minutes or until bottoms are lightly browned. Transfer cookies to a wire rack to cool. Repeat with remaining dough.

For icing, combine confectioners sugar, shortening, butter, almond extract, and 3 tablespoons milk in a large bowl; beat until smooth. If needed to thin icing, add

Made without leavening or flour, Cinnamon-Almond Macaroons are an ideal Passover sweet. Crunchy toasted almonds are a pleasing contrast to the light, airy texture of the confections.

CINNAMON-ALMOND MACAROONS

Use kosher ingredients for Passover.

- 2¹/₄ cups sliced almonds, toasted
- ¹/₂ teaspoon ground cinnamon
- 3 large egg whites
- ³/₄ cup superfine granulated sugar

Preheat oven to 350 degrees. Place almonds in a food processor; pulse process until coarsely chopped. Remove 3 tablespoons almonds; set aside. Add cinnamon to processor; process until almonds are finely ground. In a medium bowl, beat egg whites until soft peaks form.

Gradually add sugar, beating until mixture is very stiff. Gently fold ground almonds into egg white mixture. Drop rounded teaspoonfuls of mixture 2 inches apart onto a baking sheet lined with parchment paper. Lightly sprinkle reserved chopped almonds onto tops of cookies. Bake 14 to 15 minutes or until edges are lightly browned. Cool cookies on parchment paper about 2 minutes; transfer to a wire rack to cool completely. Store in an airtight container.

Yield: about 4 dozen cookies

On Mother's Day, remind Mom that she's still the prettiest flower in the garden with an offering of Spring Baskets.
...e almond-flavored cookies are beautifully decorated with sprays of sweet icing posies and tan icing piped on in
...basket weave pattern.

...maining milk ¹/₂ teaspoon at a time. ...ide icing into small bowls and tint as ...lows: ¹/₄ cup yellow, ²/₃ cup blue, ²/₃ cup ...nk, ¹/₃ cup green, and remaining icing ...n. Spoon tan icing into a pastry bag fitted ...th a basket weave tip (#47). With serrated ...le of tip up, pipe basket handle onto 1 ...okie (Fig. 1).

...g. 1

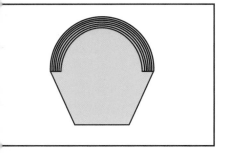

Beginning on left side of cookie, pipe a vertical stripe of frosting from middle to bottom edge of cookie. Pipe three ³/₄-inch-long horizontal stripes over vertical stripe about 1 tip width apart. Overlapping ends of horizontal stripes, pipe another vertical stripe to the right of the first vertical stripe (Fig. 2a). Pipe three ³/₄-inch-long horizontal stripes about 1 tip width apart as shown in Fig. 2b.

Fig. 2a

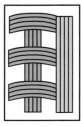

Fig. 2b

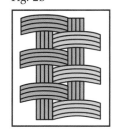

Repeat basket weave design until lower half of cookie is covered.

Use a medium drop flower tip (#131) and blue icing, and a small drop flower tip (#224) and pink icing to pipe flowers onto cookie. Use a round tip (#2) and yellow icing to pipe centers in flowers. Use a small leaf tip (#349) and green icing to pipe leaves onto flowers. Allow icing to harden. Repeat for remaining cookies. Store in single layers between sheets of waxed paper in an airtight container.

Yield: about 4 dozen cookies

SUMMER DELIGHTS

Summertime means fun-filled family picnics and excursions to the beach. When you want to take some sweet temptations along, this collection of cookies packs up in a jiffy and offers an array of scrumptious tastes. You'll find cookies that reflect the things we like best about the season, like bouquets of flowers and sweet, juicy watermelons, along with other flavorful treats to help you celebrate the summer holidays. And when you want to stay at home and entertain, you'll find a trio of goodies guaranteed to give your gatherings tropical flair. Enjoy the sunshine!

Black-eyed Susans	Hawaiian Luau Cookies
Butterscotch Brownies	Tropical Key Lime Bars
Banana-Nut Cookies	Nutty Coconut Bars
Chunky Chocolate Cookies	Mocha-Almond Bars
Watermelon Slices	Nutty Bow Ties
Chocolate-Dipped Orange Melts	Peanut Butter-Filled Chocolate Buttons

Patriotic Ribbons

(Previous page) *Perfect picnic fare, Chunky Chocolate Cookies and Banana-Nut Cookies (both in jar) are rich, chewy desserts that are filled with nutty flavor. Butterscotch Brownies (bottom) are named for their sweet, mellow blending of butter and brown sugar. Sunny reflections of the season, Black-eyed Susans get their bold centers from chocolate sprinkles. Chocolate chip "seeds" make our Watermelon Slices melt-in-your-mouth good!*

BLACK-EYED SUSANS

    1   cup butter or margarine, softened
  1/2   cup granulated sugar
  1/2   cup firmly packed brown sugar
    1   egg
    2   tablespoons grated orange zest
  1/2   teaspoon orange extract
  1/2   teaspoon vanilla extract
        Yellow paste food coloring
    2   cups all-purpose flour
  1/2   teaspoon baking soda
  1/2   teaspoon cream of tartar
        Chocolate sprinkles

In a large bowl, cream butter and sugars until fluffy. Add egg, orange zest, and extracts; beat until smooth. Tint yellow. In a small bowl, combine flour, baking soda, and cream of tartar. Add dry ingredients to creamed mixture; stir until a soft dough forms. Divide dough in half. Wrap in plastic wrap and chill 1 to 2 hours.

Preheat oven to 350 degrees. On a lightly floured surface use a floured rolling pin to roll out half of dough to 1/4-inch thickness. Use a 3-inch flower-shaped cookie cutter to cut out cookies. Place 2 inches apart on an ungreased baking sheet. Place chocolate sprinkles in centers of cookies. Bake 7 to 9 minutes or until edges are lightly browned. Transfer cookies to a wire rack to cool. Repeat with remaining dough and sprinkles. Store in an airtight container.

Yield: about 3 dozen cookies

BUTTERSCOTCH BROWNIES

  1/2   cup butter or margarine, softened
    2   cups firmly packed brown sugar
    2   eggs
 1 1/2 teaspoons vanilla extract
 1 3/4 cups all-purpose flour
 1 1/2 teaspoons baking powder
  1/2   teaspoon baking soda
  1/4   teaspoon salt
    1   cup chopped pecans, toasted

Preheat oven to 350 degrees. In a large bowl, cream butter and brown sugar until fluffy. Add eggs and vanilla; beat until smooth. In a small bowl, combine flour, baking powder, baking soda, and salt. Add dry ingredients to creamed mixture; stir until well blended. Stir in pecans. Spread batter into a lightly greased 9 x 13-inch baking pan. Bake 25 to 30 minutes or until brownies start to pull away from sides of pan. Cool in pan 15 minutes. Cut warm brownies into 2-inch squares; cool completely in pan. Store in an airtight container.

Yield: about 2 dozen brownies

BANANA-NUT COOKIES

  1/2   cup butter or margarine, softened
    1   cup granulated sugar
  1/2   cup firmly packed brown sugar
 1 1/2 cups mashed bananas (about
            3 large bananas)
    2   eggs
    1   teaspoon vanilla extract
 2 1/2 cups all-purpose flour
    2   teaspoons baking powder
    1   teaspoon ground cinnamon
  1/2   teaspoon baking soda
  1/2   teaspoon salt
    2   cups coarsely chopped walnuts

Preheat oven to 375 degrees. In a large bowl, cream butter and sugars until fluffy. Add bananas, eggs, and vanilla; beat until smooth. In a medium bowl, combine flour, baking powder, cinnamon, baking soda, and salt. Add dry ingredients to creamed mixture; stir until a soft dough forms. Stir in walnuts. Drop teaspoonfuls of dough 3 inches apart onto a greased baking sheet. Bake 8 to 10 minutes or until edges are lightly browned. Transfer cookies to a wire rack to cool. Store in an airtight container.

Yield: about 7 dozen cookies

CHUNKY CHOCOLATE COOKIES

    1   cup butter or margarine, softened
  3/4   cup firmly packed brown sugar
  1/2   cup granulated sugar
    1   egg
    1   teaspoon vanilla extract
 1 3/4 cups all-purpose flour
  1/4   cup cocoa
  1/2   teaspoon baking powder
  1/2   teaspoon baking soda
  1/2   teaspoon salt
    1   package (10 ounces) milk
            chocolate chunks
  1/2   cup chopped pecans

Preheat oven to 375 degrees. In a large bowl, cream butter and sugars until fluffy. Add egg and vanilla; beat until smooth. In a small bowl, combine flour, cocoa, baking powder, baking soda, and salt. Add dry ingredients to creamed mixture; stir until a soft dough forms. Stir in chocolate chunks and pecans. Drop tablespoonfuls of dough 2 inches apart onto an ungreased baking sheet. Bake 6 to 8 minutes or until cookies are set and bottoms are lightly browned. Transfer cookies to a wire rack to cool. Store in an airtight container.

Yield: about 4 1/2 dozen cookies

Thin and crispy, Chocolate-Dipped Orange Melts are flavored with the tangy ~~ta~~ste of oranges. Decorated with dried orange slices and a napkin trimmed with ~~co~~ordinating rickrack, our serving basket hints at the cookies' fruity taste.

WATERMELON SLICES

~~1~~/2 cups butter or margarine,
    softened
1 cup granulated sugar
2 packages (3 ounces each)
    watermelon-flavored gelatin
1 egg
1 teaspoon vanilla extract
    Pink paste food coloring
1/4 cups all-purpose flour
1/4 cup cornstarch
1 teaspoon baking powder
1 cup semisweet chocolate mini
    chips
5 tablespoons green decorating
    sugar
5 teaspoons yellow decorating sugar

In a large bowl, cream butter, granulated ~~su~~gar, and gelatin until fluffy. Add egg and

vanilla; beat until smooth. Tint pink. In a medium bowl, combine flour, cornstarch, and baking powder. Add dry ingredients to creamed mixture; stir until a soft dough forms. Stir in chocolate chips. Shape dough into four 8-inch-long rolls. Wrap in plastic wrap and chill 2 hours.

Preheat oven to 350 degrees. In a small bowl, combine decorating sugars. Roll each roll in decorating sugar. Cut dough into 1/2-inch slices. Place 2 inches apart on a greased baking sheet. Bake 10 to 12 minutes or until bottoms are lightly browned. Transfer cookies to a wire rack to cool. Store in an airtight container.

Yield: about 6½ dozen cookies

CHOCOLATE-DIPPED ORANGE MELTS

1 cup butter or margarine, softened
1 cup sugar
1 egg
1 teaspoon orange extract, divided
1/2 teaspoon vanilla extract
2¼ cups all-purpose flour
1 teaspoon baking powder
1/4 teaspoon salt
    Sugar
1 package (12 ounces) semisweet
    chocolate chips
1 tablespoon vegetable shortening

Preheat oven to 375 degrees. In a large bowl, cream butter and 1 cup sugar until fluffy. Add egg, 1/2 teaspoon orange extract, and vanilla; beat until smooth. In a medium bowl, combine flour, baking powder, and salt. Add dry ingredients to creamed mixture; stir until a soft dough forms. Shape teaspoonfuls of dough into balls and place 2 inches apart on an ungreased baking sheet. Flatten balls with bottom of a glass dipped in sugar. Bake 5 to 7 minutes or until edges are lightly browned. Transfer cookies to a wire rack to cool.

In a small saucepan, melt chocolate chips and shortening over low heat, stirring constantly. Remove from heat. Stir in remaining 1/2 teaspoon orange extract. Dip half of each cookie into melted chocolate. Place cookies on a baking sheet lined with waxed paper. Chill cookies to allow chocolate to harden. Place in single layers between sheets of waxed paper in an airtight container. Store in a cool place.

Yield: about 6 dozen cookies

HAWAIIAN LUAU COOKIES

- 1/2 cup butter or margarine, softened
- 1/2 cup granulated sugar
- 1/2 cup firmly packed brown sugar
- 1 egg
- 1/2 teaspoon vanilla extract
- 1 can (8 ounces) crushed pineapple, drained
- 2 cups all-purpose flour
- 1 teaspoon baking powder
- 1/2 teaspoon baking soda
- 1/4 teaspoon salt
- 1 cup macadamia nuts, toasted and coarsely chopped
- 1 cup sweetened shredded coconut

Preheat oven to 375 degrees. In a large bowl, cream butter and sugars until fluffy. Add egg and vanilla; beat until smooth. Stir in pineapple. In a small bowl, combine flour, baking powder, baking soda, and salt. Add dry ingredients to creamed mixture; stir until a soft dough forms. Stir in macadamia nuts and coconut. Drop tablespoonfuls of dough 2 inches apart onto a lightly greased baking sheet. Bake 8 to 10 minutes or until edges are lightly browned. Transfer cookies to a wire rack to cool. Store in an airtight container.

Yield: about 4 dozen cookies

TROPICAL KEY LIME BARS

CRUST
- 3/4 cup slivered almonds, toasted
- 1 1/4 cups all-purpose flour
- 3/4 cup sweetened finely shredded coconut
- 1/2 cup sifted confectioners sugar
- 1 cup butter or margarine, softened

FILLING
- 1 3/4 cups sugar
- 4 eggs, beaten
- 1/3 cup key lime juice
- 1 drop liquid green food coloring

Give your summertime parties a tropical climate with Hawaiian Luau Cookies (top) — *a concoction of macadamia nuts, crushed pineapple, and shredded coconut* — *and Tropical Key Lime Bars, a moist, zippy surprise. Drizzled with icing, Nutty Coconut Bars* (right) *have a coconut-pecan filling that's just sensational!*

- 1/4 cup all-purpose flour
- 1/4 teaspoon baking powder

Preheat oven to 350 degrees. For crust, place almonds in a food processor; process until almost finely ground. Add flour, coconut, and confectioners sugar; pulse process until well blended. Add butter; continue to process until a soft dough forms. Spread into bottom and 1/4 inch up sides of a greased 9 x 13-inch baking pan. Bake 20 minutes.

For filling, combine first 4 ingredients in a medium bowl; whisk until well blended. In a small bowl, combine flour and baking powder. Add dry ingredients to sugar mixture; whisk until well blended. Pour mixture over crust. Return to oven and bake 25 to 30 minutes or until filling is set. Cool in pan. Cut into 1 x 2-inch bars. Store in a single layer in an airtight container.

Yield: about 4 dozen bars

[NU]TTY COCONUT BARS

[CR]UST

1 cup all-purpose flour
½ cup butter or margarine, softened

[FIL]LING

[1]¼ cups firmly packed brown sugar
[1]½ cups chopped pecans
½ cup sweetened shredded coconut
2 eggs
1 tablespoon butter or margarine, melted
¼ teaspoon baking powder

[ICI]NG

½ cup sifted confectioners sugar
2 teaspoons milk
½ teaspoon vanilla extract

[P]reheat oven to 350 degrees. For crust, [com]bine flour and butter in a small bowl [unt]il well blended. Line a 9 x 13-inch [ba]king pan with a double layer of aluminum [foil], extending foil over ends of pan; grease [foil]. Press dough into bottom of prepared [pan]. Bake 15 minutes.

[F]or filling, combine brown sugar, [pec]ans, and coconut in a medium bowl. In [a s]mall bowl, whisk eggs, butter, and baking [pow]der until well blended. Add to brown [sug]ar mixture; stir until well blended. [Spr]ead over hot crust. Bake 18 to [22] minutes or until set in center. Place pan [on] a wire rack to cool.

[F]or icing, combine all ingredients in a [sm]all bowl; stir until smooth. Drizzle icing [ove]r top. Allow icing to harden. Lift from [pan] using ends of foil. Cut into 1 x 2-inch [bar]s. Store in an airtight container.

[Yie]ld: about 4 dozen bars

Mocha-Almond Bars will perk up your day, especially when they're enjoyed with a fresh cup of coffee. Semisweet chocolate and instant coffee, combined with the subtle flavor of almonds, give the bars their rich charm.

MOCHA-ALMOND BARS

1 cup butter or margarine, softened
1 cup firmly packed brown sugar
1 teaspoon almond extract
2 cups all-purpose flour
2 tablespoons instant coffee granules
½ teaspoon baking powder
¼ teaspoon salt
1 package (6 ounces) semisweet chocolate chips
¾ cup sliced almonds, toasted and coarsely chopped

Preheat oven to 350 degrees. In a large bowl, cream butter, brown sugar, and almond extract until fluffy. In a small bowl, combine flour, coffee granules, baking powder, and salt. Add dry ingredients to creamed mixture; stir until a soft dough forms. Stir in chocolate chips and almonds. Press mixture into an ungreased 10½ x 15½-inch jellyroll pan. Bake 15 to 20 minutes or until lightly browned on top. Cool in pan 5 minutes. Cut into 1 x 2-inch bars while warm; cool completely in pan. Store in an airtight container.

Yield: about 5 dozen bars

On Father's Day, wrap up a batch of Peanut Butter-Filled Chocolate Buttons, luscious snacks that resemble Dad's blazer buttons. And don't forget to include a collection of Nutty Bow Ties — they're striped with food coloring and shaped into tasty little "bow ties." Dad is sure to love trying them on for size!

NUTTY BOW TIES

- ¹/₂ cup butter or margarine, softened
- ¹/₄ cup vegetable shortening
- 1¹/₄ cups firmly packed brown sugar
- 1 egg
- 1 teaspoon vanilla-butter-nut flavoring
- 2¹/₄ cups all-purpose flour
- ¹/₂ teaspoon baking soda
- ¹/₄ teaspoon salt
- ³/₄ cup chopped pecans, toasted and finely ground
  Red and blue liquid food coloring

In a large bowl, cream butter, shortening, and brown sugar until fluffy. Add egg and vanilla-butter-nut flavoring; beat until smooth. In a medium bowl, combine flour, baking soda, and salt. Add dry ingredients to creamed mixture; stir until a soft dough forms. Stir in pecans. Divide dough in half. Wrap in plastic wrap and chill 2 hours.

Preheat oven to 375 degrees. On a lightly floured surface, use a floured rolling pin to roll out half of dough into a 9 x 12-inch rectangle. Use food coloring to paint diagonal stripes across dough. Cut out 1¹/₂ x 3-inch rectangles of dough. Place 2 inches apart on an ungreased baking sheet. On each cookie, squeeze center of long edges toward middle to create "knot" in tie. Bake 8 to 10 minutes or until bottoms are lightly browned. Transfer to a wire rack to cool. Repeat with remaining dough. Store in an airtight container.

Yield: 4 dozen cookies

PEANUT BUTTER-FILLED CHOCOLATE BUTTONS

- 1¹/₄ cups butter or margarine, softened
- 1 cup sugar
- 1 egg
- 2 tablespoons milk
- 1 teaspoon vanilla extract
- 2¹/₂ cups all-purpose flour
- ¹/₂ cup cocoa
- ³/₄ teaspoon baking powder
- ¹/₄ teaspoon baking soda
- ³/₄ cup smooth peanut butter

In a large bowl, cream butter and sugar until fluffy. Add egg, milk, and vanilla; beat until smooth. In a medium bowl, combine flour, cocoa, baking powder, and baking soda. Add dry ingredients to creamed

ture; stir until a soft dough forms. Cover
 chill 2 hours or until firm enough to
 dle.

reheat oven to 350 degrees. Shape
 gh into 1-inch balls and place 1 inch
 rt on an ungreased baking sheet. Use
 er to make an indentation in the center
 ach cookie. Spoon peanut butter into a
 try bag fitted with a large round tip. Pipe
 nall amount of peanut butter into center
 ach cookie. Bake 6 to 8 minutes or until
 toms are browned. Cool cookies on pan
 inutes; transfer to a wire rack to cool
 npletely. Store in single layers between
 ets of waxed paper in an airtight
 tainer.

 ld: about 7 1/2 dozen cookies

TRIOTIC RIBBONS

 1 cup butter or margarine, softened
 /4 cups sugar
 1 egg
 1 teaspoon vanilla extract
 /2 cups all-purpose flour
 /2 teaspoons baking powder
 /2 teaspoon salt
 1 cup chopped pecans, toasted and
       finely ground
 /4 teaspoon *each* red and blue paste
       food coloring

 n a large bowl, cream butter and sugar
 l fluffy. Add egg and vanilla; beat until
 oth. In a medium bowl, combine flour,
 ing powder, and salt. Add dry
 redients to creamed mixture; stir until a
 t dough forms. Stir in pecans. Divide
 gh into thirds. Tint one third of dough
 . and one third of dough blue. Line a
 12-inch baking pan with waxed paper,
 ending paper over long sides; lightly
 ase paper. Press blue dough into bottom
 an. Press plain dough over blue dough.
 ss red dough over plain dough. Cover
 with plastic wrap and chill overnight.

*Drum up some spirit on the Fourth of July with these Patriotic Ribbons!
Fun to make, the cookies are simply layers of tinted dough that are chilled and
cut into "ribbons" before baking.*

Preheat oven to 375 degrees. Run a knife
along ends of pan to loosen dough. Use
ends of waxed paper to lift dough from pan.
Cut dough into 1/8-inch slices. Place
2 inches apart on an ungreased nonstick
baking sheet. Bake 8 to 10 minutes or until
bottoms are lightly browned. Transfer
cookies to a wire rack to cool. Store in an
airtight container.

Yield: about 4 dozen cookies

AUTUMN HARVEST

Baking cookies is a wonderful way to warm your home during the crisp, cool days of autumn. And this colorful sampling contains a variety of cookies that lets you enjoy the harvest season's ample supply of fruits and grains. You'll find cookies that reflect fall's glorious foliage, along with fun-filled goodies for Halloween and some treats for which your family will truly be thankful. When you want to fill the cookie jar with the bounty of the season, turn to this sweet collection. It's simply spectacular!

(Previous page) Make your harvest celebrations sweeter by dressing your table with Maple-Nut Wreaths (in pumpkin), pretty pie-like cookies with a nutty filling. A rich and creamy butterscotch topping enhances our Walnut Spice Bars (left), which have a moist, spicy crust. Semisweet baking chocolate gives Buttery Spirals their colorful swirls.

MAPLE-NUT WREATHS

    1   cup butter or margarine, softened
  1/2   cup sugar
    1   egg
    1   teaspoon vanilla extract
  21/2 cups all-purpose flour
    2   cups chopped pecans, toasted and
          finely ground
  1/2   cup maple syrup

Preheat oven to 350 degrees. In a large bowl, cream butter and sugar until fluffy. Add egg and vanilla; beat until smooth. Add flour; stir until a soft dough forms. Place 1/2 cup dough in a small bowl; set aside. Place remaining dough in a cookie press fitted with a star plate. Press dough into 4-inch lengths onto a baking sheet lined with parchment paper. Join ends of each dough length to form a wreath. Add pecans and maple syrup to reserved dough; stir until well blended. Place 1 teaspoon pecan mixture in center of each wreath. Bake 10 to 15 minutes or until bottoms are lightly browned. Transfer cookies to a wire rack to cool. Store in an airtight container.

Yield: about 5 dozen cookies

WALNUT SPICE BARS

CRUST
    1   package (18.25 ounces) spice
          cake mix
  1/3   cup vegetable oil
  1/3   cup applesauce
    1   egg
    1   teaspoon vanilla extract
TOPPING
    1   cup sugar
  1/3   cup butter or margarine
  1/3   cup milk
    1   cup butterscotch chips
    1   cup chopped walnuts

Preheat oven to 350 degrees. For crust, combine cake mix, oil, applesauce, egg, and vanilla in a medium bowl. Spread mixture into bottom of a 9 x 13-inch baking pan lined with lightly greased waxed paper. Bake 20 to 25 minutes or until edges are lightly browned. While crust is baking prepare topping.

For topping, combine sugar, butter, and milk in a heavy medium saucepan over medium-high heat. Stirring constantly, bring mixture to a boil and boil 1 minute. Remove from heat and add butterscotch chips; stir until smooth. Stir in walnuts. Spread hot topping over warm crust. Cool in pan. Cut into 1 x 2-inch bars. Store in an airtight container.

Yield: about 4 dozen bars

BUTTERY SPIRALS

  11/2 cups all-purpose flour
    1   cup chilled butter
  1/2   cup sour cream
    1   teaspoon vanilla extract
    2   ounces semisweet baking
          chocolate, melted
        Sugar

Place flour in a medium bowl. Using a pastry blender or 2 knives, cut in butter

until mixture resembles coarse meal. Stir sour cream and vanilla. Divide dough in half. Add melted chocolate to half of doug Divide plain and chocolate doughs in half Wrap in plastic wrap and chill 2 hours.

Between pieces of plastic wrap sprinkle with sugar, roll out half of plain dough int a 6 x 10-inch rectangle. Repeat to roll ou half of chocolate dough. Using plastic wra place chocolate dough on top of plain dough. Beginning at 1 long edge, roll up dough jellyroll style. Wrap roll in plastic wrap. Repeat with remaining doughs. Chi 1 hour.

Preheat oven to 375 degrees. Cut doug into 1/2-inch slices. Place 2 inches apart o a baking sheet lined with parchment pape Lightly sprinkle cookies with sugar. Bake 12 minutes. Turn cookies over, sprinkle with sugar, and bake an additional 2 to 3 minutes. Transfer cookies to a wire rac to cool. Store in an airtight container.

Yield: about 3 dozen cookies

MAPLE LEAVES

    1   cup butter or margarine, softened
  2/3   cup vegetable shortening
    2   cups sugar
  1/2   cup maple syrup
    2   eggs
    1   teaspoon maple flavoring
    1   teaspoon vanilla extract
    6   cups all-purpose flour
  1/2   teaspoon salt
    6   tablespoons water
        Orange, green, yellow, copper,
          brown, and red paste food
          coloring

Preheat oven to 350 degrees. In a large bowl, cream butter, shortening, and suga until fluffy. Add syrup, eggs, maple flavori and vanilla; beat until smooth. In another large bowl, combine flour and salt. Add d ingredients to creamed mixture; stir until soft dough forms.

Why not bake up a basketful of Maple Leaves in honor of the glorious fall foliage! Fashioned with a cookie cutter, the brilliant "leaves" are shaded with diluted food coloring.

On a lightly floured surface, use a floured rolling pin to roll out dough to ¼-inch thickness. Use a 3 x 2½-inch maple leaf-shaped cookie cutter to cut out cookies. Transfer to a greased baking sheet. Bake 7 to 9 minutes or until bottoms are lightly browned. Transfer cookies to a wire rack to cool.

Place 1 tablespoon water in each of 6 small bowls. Tint each bowl of water with a small amount of food coloring. To decorate cookies, use a small paintbrush to lightly brush diluted food coloring onto cookies to resemble fall leaves. Allow to dry. Store in an airtight container.

Yield: about 9 dozen cookies

ORANGE-WALNUT COOKIES

COOKIES

- 1/2 cup butter or margarine, softened
- 2/3 cup sugar
- 1 egg
- 1 teaspoon vanilla extract
- 1 teaspoon orange extract
- 6 tablespoons orange marmalade
- 1 3/4 cups all-purpose flour
- 1 1/4 teaspoons baking powder
- 1/8 teaspoon salt
- 3/4 cup finely chopped toasted walnuts

GLAZE

- 1 1/2 cups sifted confectioners sugar
- 3 tablespoons orange marmalade
- 1 tablespoon milk
- 3/4 teaspoon orange extract

Preheat oven to 375 degrees. For cookies, cream butter and sugar in a large bowl until fluffy. Add egg and extracts; beat until smooth. Stir in marmalade. In a small bowl, combine flour, baking powder, and salt. Add dry ingredients to creamed mixture; stir until a soft dough forms. Stir in walnuts. Drop tablespoonfuls of dough 2 inches apart onto a greased baking sheet. Bake 7 to 9 minutes or until edges are lightly browned. Transfer cookies to a wire rack to cool.

For glaze, combine all ingredients in a small bowl; stir until smooth. Spread glaze on tops of cookies. Allow glaze to harden. Store in an airtight container.

Yield: about 3 dozen cookies

RAISIN CRUNCH COOKIES

- 3/4 cup butter or margarine, softened
- 3/4 cup firmly packed brown sugar
- 3/4 cup granulated sugar
- 1 egg
- 1 teaspoon vanilla extract
- 1 1/2 cups all-purpose flour
- 1/2 teaspoon baking soda

- 1/2 teaspoon baking powder
- 2 cups crushed corn flake cereal
- 1 cup quick-cooking oats
- 1 cup sweetened shredded coconut
- 1 cup raisins

Preheat oven to 350 degrees. In a large bowl, cream butter and sugars until fluffy. Add egg and vanilla; beat until smooth. In a small bowl, combine flour, baking soda, and baking powder. Add dry ingredients to creamed mixture; stir until a soft dough forms. Stir in remaining ingredients. Drop tablespoonfuls of dough 2 inches apart on an ungreased baking sheet. Bake 8 to 10 minutes or until edges are lightly browned. Transfer cookies to a wire rack cool. Store in an airtight container.

Yield: about 5 dozen cookies

Marmalade adds moistness and zest to Orange-Walnut Cookies (left), *soft morsels filled with chopped walnuts and topped with a fruity glaze. Raisin Crunch Cookies offer a potpourri of tastes — they're made with crushed corn flakes, quick-cooking oats, shredded coconut, and sweet raisins.*

Brew up some Halloween treats for your guests with a batch of Orange Slice Cookies. They're made with sliced gumdrop candies for a delicious surprise!

ORANGE SLICE COOKIES

3/4 cup butter or margarine, softened
  1 cup granulated sugar
1/2 cup firmly packed brown sugar
  1 egg
  1 teaspoon vanilla extract
3/4 cups all-purpose flour
1/2 teaspoon baking powder
1/2 teaspoon salt
  2 cups (about 1 pound) orange
     slice gumdrop candies,
     quartered

In a large bowl, cream butter and sugars until fluffy. Add egg and vanilla; beat until smooth. In a small bowl, combine flour, baking powder, and salt. Add dry ingredients to creamed mixture; stir until a soft dough forms. Stir in candy pieces. Shape dough into three 9-inch-long rolls. Wrap in plastic wrap and chill 3 hours or until firm enough to handle.

Preheat oven to 375 degrees. Cut dough into 1/4-inch slices. Place 1 inch apart on a lightly greased baking sheet. Bake 6 to 8 minutes or until edges are lightly browned. Transfer cookies to a wire rack to cool. Store in an airtight container.

Yield: about 6 dozen cookies

SPICED PUMPKIN COOKIES

COOKIES

- ½ cup butter or margarine, softened
- 1½ cups firmly packed brown sugar
- ¾ cup canned pumpkin
- 1 egg
- 1 tablespoon grated orange zest
- 1¼ cups all-purpose flour
- 1¼ cups whole-wheat flour
- 1 teaspoon pumpkin pie spice
- 1 teaspoon baking soda
- ¼ teaspoon salt
- 2 cups chopped walnuts

ICING

- ½ cup butter or margarine
- 1 cup firmly packed brown sugar
- ¼ cup whipping cream
- 1 tablespoon light corn syrup
- 1 cup sifted confectioners sugar

For cookies, cream butter and brown sugar in a large bowl until fluffy. Add pumpkin, egg, and orange zest; beat until smooth. In a medium bowl, combine flours, pumpkin pie spice, baking soda, and salt. Add dry ingredients to creamed mixture; stir until a soft dough forms. Stir in walnuts. Wrap in plastic wrap and chill 4 hours.

Preheat oven to 375 degrees. Drop tablespoonfuls of dough 2 inches apart onto a greased baking sheet. Bake 10 to 12 minutes or until bottoms are lightly browned. Transfer cookies to a wire rack to cool.

For icing, melt butter in a heavy medium saucepan over medium heat. Stirring constantly, add brown sugar, whipping cream, and corn syrup; cook until mixture comes to a boil. Boil 1 minute. Remove from heat; pour into a heat-resistant medium bowl. Add confectioners sugar and beat until smooth. Ice cookies. Allow icing to harden. Store in an airtight container.

Yield: about 5 dozen cookies

Served with a steaming cup of hot cocoa, Chocolate Crinkle Cookies (left) will hit the spot on a cool autumn day. The chocolaty delights, dropped in confectioners sugar before baking, pair nicely with Spiced Pumpkin Cookies, seasonal goodies that are topped with a creamy icing.

CHOCOLATE CRINKLE COOKIES

1/2 cup butter or margarine, softened
2 cups granulated sugar
6 ounces semisweet baking
    chocolate, melted
4 eggs
2 teaspoons vanilla extract
2 cups all-purpose flour
2 teaspoons baking powder
1/2 teaspoon salt
1 cup sifted confectioners sugar

In a large bowl, combine butter, granulated sugar, and melted chocolate; beat until well blended. Add eggs, 1 at a time, beating well after each addition. Add vanilla, continuing to beat until smooth. In a small bowl, combine flour, baking powder, and salt. Add dry ingredients to creamed mixture; stir until well blended. Cover dough and chill 4 hours.

Preheat oven to 350 degrees. Place confectioners sugar in a small bowl. Drop teaspoonfuls of dough into confectioners sugar. Shape into 1-inch balls, using sugar to keep dough from sticking to hands. Place balls 3 inches apart on a baking sheet lined with parchment paper. Bake 7 to 9 minutes or until edges are firm. Transfer cookies to a wire rack to cool. Store in an airtight container.

Yield: about 7 1/2 dozen cookies

PUMPKIN COOKIE POPS

3/4 cup butter or margarine, softened
    and divided
1 package (3 ounces) cream cheese,
    softened
1 cup sugar
1 egg
1 teaspoon orange extract
1/2 teaspoon vanilla extract
    Orange paste food coloring
2 3/4 cups all-purpose flour, divided
1 teaspoon baking powder

Baked on lollipop sticks, orange-flavored Pumpkin Cookie Pops offer a spirited way to serve up some Halloween fun. The spellbinding treats, fashioned with cookie cutters, get their friendly faces from baked-on chocolate batter.

1/4 teaspoon salt
    Lollipop sticks
1 tablespoon chocolate syrup

In a large bowl, cream 1/2 cup butter, cream cheese, and sugar until fluffy. Add egg and extracts; beat until smooth. Tint orange. In a medium bowl, combine 2 1/2 cups flour, baking powder, and salt. Add dry ingredients to creamed mixture; stir until a soft dough forms. Divide dough in half. Wrap in plastic wrap and chill 2 hours.

Preheat oven to 350 degrees. On a lightly floured surface, use a floured rolling pin to roll out half of dough to 3/8-inch thickness. Use a 2 1/4-inch-diameter pumpkin-shaped cookie cutter to cut out cookies. Transfer to a lightly greased baking sheet. Carefully insert lollipop sticks into bottoms of cookies. In a small bowl, combine remaining 1/4 cup butter, remaining 1/4 cup flour, and chocolate syrup; stir until well blended. Spoon chocolate mixture into a pastry bag fitted with a small round tip. Pipe a pumpkin face onto each cookie. Bake 8 to 10 minutes or until bottoms are lightly browned. Transfer cookies to a wire rack to cool. Repeat with remaining dough. Store in an airtight container.

Yield: about 2 1/2 dozen cookies

HONEY-NUT DROPS

1/2 cup butter or margarine, softened
3/4 cup firmly packed brown sugar
1/2 cup honey
1 egg
1/2 teaspoon vanilla extract
2 cups all-purpose flour
1 teaspoon baking powder
1/4 teaspoon salt
1 cup coarsely chopped toasted
pecans
Granulated sugar

Preheat oven to 350 degrees. In a large bowl, cream butter and brown sugar until fluffy. Add honey, egg, and vanilla; beat until smooth. In a small bowl, combine flour, baking powder, and salt. Add dry ingredients to creamed mixture; stir until a soft dough forms. Stir in pecans. Drop teaspoonfuls of dough 2 inches apart onto a lightly greased baking sheet; flatten with bottom of a glass dipped in granulated sugar. Bake 6 to 9 minutes or until bottoms are lightly browned. Transfer cookies to a wire rack to cool. Store in a cookie tin.

Yield: about 6 1/2 dozen cookies

CHERRY-OAT-NUT SQUARES

3/4 cup butter or margarine, softened
1 cup firmly packed brown sugar
1 1/2 cups quick-cooking oats
1 1/4 cups all-purpose flour
1/2 teaspoon baking soda
1/4 teaspoon salt
1 can (21 ounces) cherry pie
filling
1 package (3 ounces) cream
cheese, softened
1 egg
1 1/2 cups sifted confectioners sugar
1 teaspoon vanilla extract
1/2 teaspoon ground cinnamon
1/8 teaspoon ground nutmeg
1 cup finely chopped toasted pecans

A Thanksgiving feast traditionally includes mouth-watering desserts like Honey-Nut Drops (in basket), cookies bursting with nutty goodness, and Cherry-Oat-Nut Squares, moist sweets that are created with cherry pie filling, cream cheese, and nuts.

Preheat oven to 350 degrees. In a medium bowl, cream butter and brown sugar until fluffy. In a small bowl, combine oats, flour, baking soda, and salt. Add dry ingredients to creamed mixture; stir until well blended. Reserving 1/2 cup oat mixture, firmly press remainder of mixture into bottom of a lightly greased 9 x 13-inch baking pan. Spread cherry pie filling over crust. In a medium bowl, beat cream cheese and egg. Add confectioners sugar, vanilla, cinnamon, and nutmeg; beat until smooth. Stir in pecans. Spread cream cheese mixture over cherries. Crumble reserved oat mixture over cream cheese mixture. Bake 40 to 45 minutes or until center is set and top is lightly browned. Cool in pan. Cut into 1 1/2-inch squares. Store in an airtight container in refrigerator.

Yield: about 4 dozen squares

DATE-FILLED PINWHEELS

COOKIES

- 1 cup butter or margarine, softened
- 1 cup granulated sugar
- 1 cup firmly packed brown sugar
- 3 eggs
- 1/2 teaspoon vanilla extract
- 1/2 cups all-purpose flour
- 1 teaspoon baking soda
- 1 teaspoon ground cinnamon
- 1/4 teaspoon salt

FILLING

- 12 ounces dates, finely chopped
- 6 tablespoons sugar
- 6 tablespoons orange juice
- 2 teaspoons grated orange zest

For cookies, cream butter and sugars until fluffy. Add eggs and vanilla; beat until smooth. In a medium bowl, combine dry ingredients and add to creamed mixture; stir until a soft dough forms. Divide dough into fourths. Wrap in plastic wrap and chill.

For filling, combine all ingredients in a heavy medium saucepan over medium heat. Stirring frequently, cook 8 minutes or until mixture thickens. Remove from heat.

On a well floured surface, use a floured rolling pin to roll out one fourth of dough to 8-inch thickness. Using a pastry wheel, cut dough into 2 1/2-inch squares; place 1 inch apart on a greased baking sheet. Use pastry wheel make a 1-inch cut from each corner toward the center of each square. Place 2 teaspoon of date mixture in center of square. Bring every other dough corner toward the center of cookie, leaving filling uncovered; press into place at edge of filling. Repeat with remaining dough. Chill cookies 45 minutes.

Preheat oven to 350 degrees. Bake 6 to minutes or until edges are lightly browned. Transfer cookies to a wire rack to cool. Store in an airtight container.

Yield: about 6 dozen cookies

Shaped like one of our favorite childhood toys, Date-Filled Pinwheels are soft cookies flavored with a hint of cinnamon. The cookies, filled with a fruity blend of dates and orange juice, feature pretty edges created using a pastry wheel.

CHRISTMAS FAVORITES

The Christmas season brings a flurry of activities, and baking cookies is one of our favorite traditions. There's just something about creating — and sharing — home-baked goodies that fills us with the holiday spirit. And of course, it's only fitting that we should treat Santa to a sampling of sweets, too! The cookies in this festive collection capture the magic of the season, making all your Yuletide gatherings with friends and family especially sweet.

Christmas Jewels	Spiked Eggnog Brownies
"Merry Christmas" Cookies	Spiced Christmas Stars
Christmas Macaroons	Stained Glass Cookies
Chocolate Fruitcake Cookies	Pineapple Jumbles
Chewy Fruitcake Bars	Tasty Christmas Wreaths

(Previous page) Our "Merry Christmas" Cookies, fashioned with alphabet cookie cutters and decorated with colorful icing, offer a fun way to greet your guests with a holiday message. Christmas Jewels (in jar) are buttery piped cookies that get their sparkle from red and green gumdrops.

CHRISTMAS JEWELS

1 1/2   cups butter or margarine,
        softened
1   cup sugar
1   egg
2   teaspoons vanilla extract
3   cups all-purpose flour
1   teaspoon baking powder
    Small red and green gumdrops

Preheat oven to 400 degrees. In a large bowl, cream butter and sugar until fluffy. Add egg and vanilla; beat until smooth. In a medium bowl, combine flour and baking powder. Add dry ingredients to creamed mixture; stir until a soft dough forms. Spoon mixture into a pastry bag fitted with a large open star tip. Pipe 2-inch-long shells onto a greased baking sheet lined with parchment paper. Press a gumdrop into small end of each shell. Bake 6 to 8 minutes or until bottoms are lightly browned. Transfer cookies to a wire rack to cool. Store in an airtight container.

Yield: about 6 dozen cookies

"MERRY CHRISTMAS" COOKIES

COOKIES

3/4   cup butter or margarine, softened
1   cup sifted confectioners sugar
1   egg
1 1/2   teaspoons almond extract
2 1/2   cups all-purpose flour
1/4   teaspoon salt

ICING

1/4   cup water
2   tablespoons light corn syrup
4   cups sifted confectioners sugar
1 1/4   teaspoons almond extract
2   to 3 teaspoons half and half
    Green and red paste food
        coloring
    Purchased green and red
        decorating icing to decorate

For cookies, cream butter and confectioners sugar in a large bowl until fluffy. Add egg and almond extract; beat until smooth. In a medium bowl, combine flour and salt. Add dry ingredients to creamed mixture; stir until a soft dough forms. Divide dough in half. Wrap in plastic wrap and chill 1 hour.

Preheat oven to 350 degrees. On a lightly floured surface, use a floured rolling pin to roll out half of dough to 1/4-inch thickness. Use 2-inch-high alphabet cookie cutters to cut out "Merry Christmas" cookies. Transfer to a greased baking sheet. Bake 8 to 10 minutes or until edges are lightly browned. Transfer cookies to a wire rack with waxed paper underneath to cool. Repeat with remaining dough.

For icing, combine water and corn syrup in a heavy medium saucepan. Add confectioners sugar and stir until well blended. Using a pastry brush dipped in hot water, wash down any sugar crystals on sides of pan. Attach a candy thermometer to pan, making sure thermometer does not touch bottom of pan. Stirring constantly and taking care not to scrape sides of pan, cook over medium-low heat until icing reaches 100 degrees. Remove from heat; stir in almond extract and 2 teaspoons half and half. Cool icing 5 minutes. Divide icing evenly into 3 small bowls; tint 1 green and 1 red. If needed, add additional half and half, 1/4 teaspoon at a time, for desired consistency. Spoon icings over letters. Allow icing to harden.

To decorate, transfer purchased green decorating icing into a pastry bag fitted with a small leaf tip. Transfer red icing into a pastry bag fitted with a very small round tip. Pipe holly leaves, berries, and candy cane stripes onto desired letters. Allow icing to harden. Store in a single layer in an airtight container.

Yield: about 5 sets of cookies

CHRISTMAS MACAROONS

1 1/4   cups sugar, divided
1/2   cup all-purpose flour
1/4   teaspoon salt
2 1/2   cups sweetened shredded
        coconut
4   egg whites
1/2   teaspoon vanilla extract
1   cup finely chopped green and red
        candied cherries

Preheat oven to 325 degrees. In a small bowl, combine 1/4 cup sugar, flour, and salt. Stir in coconut; set aside.

In a medium bowl, beat egg whites until soft peaks form. Add vanilla. Gradually add remaining 1 cup sugar, beating until mixture is very stiff. Gently fold coconut mixture and candied cherries into egg white mixture.

Drop teaspoonfuls of mixture onto a baking sheet lined with parchment paper. Bake 15 to 17 minutes or until edges are lightly browned. Transfer cookies to a wire rack to cool. Store in an airtight container.

Yield: about 5 dozen cookies

CHOCOLATE FRUITCAKE COOKIES

COOKIES

- 3/4 cup butter or margarine, softened
- 3/4 cup sugar
- 2 eggs
- 1 teaspoon vanilla extract
- 2 ounces semisweet baking chocolate, melted
- 3/4 cups all-purpose flour
- 1 teaspoon baking powder
- 1 cup coarsely chopped candied red and green cherries
- 1 cup coarsely chopped toasted pecans

GLAZE

- 1/2 cup semisweet chocolate chips
- 1 teaspoon vegetable shortening
  Green and red candied cherries to decorate

Preheat oven to 375 degrees. For cookies, cream butter and sugar in a large bowl until fluffy. Add eggs and vanilla; beat until smooth. Stir in melted chocolate. In a medium bowl, combine flour and baking powder. Add dry ingredients to creamed mixture; stir until a soft dough forms. Stir in cherries and pecans. Drop tablespoonfuls of dough 2 inches apart onto a lightly greased baking sheet. Bake 6 to 8 minutes or until bottoms are lightly browned. Transfer cookies to a wire rack to cool.

For glaze, place chocolate chips and shortening in a small microwave-safe bowl. Microwave on medium-high power (80%) 1 minute; stir. Continue to microwave 30 seconds at a time, stirring until melted. Drizzle glaze over half of cookies; decorate remaining cookies with candied cherry pieces. Store in an airtight container.

Yield: about 4 1/2 dozen cookies

Brimming with candied cherries, Christmas Macaroons (top) have traditional holiday flavor. The light and luscious cookies are great take-along fare when they're packed in a festive basket. Chocolate lovers will enjoy indulging in Chocolate Fruitcake Cookies — chewy morsels chock-full of semisweet chocolate, candied cherries, and chopped pecans.

SPIKED EGGNOG BROWNIES

BROWNIES

- 1/2 cup butter or margarine
- 1/2 cup water
- 1/2 cup vegetable oil
- 2 cups all-purpose flour
- 2 cups sugar
- 1/4 cup cocoa
- 1/2 teaspoon baking powder
- 1/8 teaspoon salt
- 1/2 cup eggnog
- 1/2 cup bourbon
- 2 eggs

ICING

- 2 cups sifted confectioners sugar
- 6 tablespoons butter or margarine, softened
- 1/4 cup vegetable shortening
- 2 tablespoons eggnog
- 2 teaspoons bourbon
- 1/8 teaspoon freshly grated nutmeg

Preheat oven to 400 degrees. For brownies, combine butter, water, and oil in a heavy small saucepan over medium-high heat. Bring to a boil. Remove from heat. In a medium bowl, combine flour, sugar, cocoa, baking powder, and salt. Add dry ingredients to butter mixture; stir until well blended. In a small bowl, whisk eggnog and bourbon into eggs; stir into batter. Pour batter into a greased 10 1/2 x 15 1/2-inch jellyroll pan lined with waxed paper. Bake 12 to 14 minutes or until a toothpick inserted near center comes out clean. Cool in pan. Cut into 2-inch squares.

For icing, combine all ingredients in a medium bowl. Beat until well blended and smooth. Spoon icing into a pastry bag fitted with a large open star tip. Pipe icing onto each brownie. Store in an airtight container in refrigerator.

Yield: about 3 dozen brownies

Chewy Fruitcake Bars (top) are packed with candied fruit, shredded coconut, and walnuts to satisfy your sweet tooth. Laced with bourbon, Spiked Eggnog Brownies are a tempting midnight snack for Santa — the extra-moist treats will warm him up after his long journey!

CHEWY FRUITCAKE BARS

- 1/2 cup butter or margarine, softened
- 1/3 cup firmly packed brown sugar
- 1 cup all-purpose flour
- 1 cup chopped walnuts
- 1 cup chopped dates
- 1 cup sweetened shredded coconut
- 1/2 cup green candied whole cherries
- 1/2 cup red candied whole cherries
- 1/2 cup candied pineapple wedges
- 1 can (14 ounces) sweetened condensed milk

Preheat oven to 350 degrees. In a large bowl, cream butter and brown sugar until fluffy. Add flour; stir until a soft dough forms. Press mixture into a greased 9 x 13-inch baking pan. Bake 10 minutes.

Place walnuts, dates, coconut, cherries, and pineapple in food processor. Pulse process until mixture is coarsely chopped. Reserve 1 cup processed fruit mixture. Spoon remaining mixture over crust. Pour sweetened condensed milk over fruit mixture. Sprinkle reserved mixture on top. Bake 30 minutes or until top is lightly browned. Cool in pan 15 minutes. Cut into 1 x 2-inch bars while warm; cool completely in pan. Store in an airtight container.

Yield: about 4 dozen bars

SPICED CHRISTMAS STARS

/2 cup butter or margarine, softened
/2 cup firmly packed brown sugar
 2 eggs
/2 cup honey
/2 cups all-purpose flour
/4 cup cornstarch
/2 teaspoons ground cinnamon
 1 teaspoon baking soda
/2 teaspoon ground ginger
/4 teaspoon ground nutmeg
/4 teaspoon salt
   Red and green candied cherries,
      halved
   Blanched whole almonds
   Walnut halves

te: Use pattern, page 118, and follow
tting Out Cookies, page 122, or use a
rchased 4-inch cookie cutter.
In a large bowl, cream butter and brown
gar until fluffy. Add eggs and honey; beat
til smooth. In a medium bowl, combine
ur, cornstarch, cinnamon, baking soda,
ger, nutmeg, and salt. Gradually add dry
redients to creamed mixture; stir until a
t dough forms. Divide dough in half.
ap in plastic wrap and chill 2 hours.
Preheat oven to 350 degrees. On a lightly
ured surface, use a floured rolling pin to
l out half of dough to 1/4-inch thickness.
t out cookies. Place 2 inches apart on a
eased baking sheet. Cut a 3/4-inch-
meter hole in center of each cookie.
corate tops of cookies with cherries and
nonds or walnuts. Bake 6 to 8 minutes or
til golden brown. Transfer cookies to a
e rack to cool. Repeat with remaining
ugh. Store in an airtight container.
ld: about 2 dozen cookies

*If you've been to Germany's famous Christkindl Market, you'll recognize
these colorful cookies. Decorated with whole almonds, candied cherries, and
walnut halves, Spiced Christmas Stars resemble a traditional Bavarian favorite.*

Festive tins invite friends and family to try a sampling of tasty treats like soft, chewy Pineapple Jumbles (left), *which offer a tropical surprise in every bite. Candied pineapple and cherries combine with chopped pecans and a sweet glaze to create pretty Stained Glass Cookies, diamond-shaped shortbread tidbits that are sure to dazzle.*

STAINED GLASS COOKIES

1	cup butter or margarine, softened
1¹/₂	cups sugar
1	egg
1	teaspoon vanilla extract
2³/₄	cups all-purpose flour
¹/₄	teaspoon salt
1	pound mixed candied fruit, coarsely chopped
2	cups chopped pecans
¹/₄	cup light corn syrup

Preheat oven to 375 degrees. In a large bowl, cream butter and sugar until fluffy. Add egg and vanilla; beat until smooth. In a medium bowl, combine flour and salt. Add dry ingredients to creamed mixture; stir until a soft dough forms. Line a

10¹/₂ x 15¹/₂-inch jellyroll pan with heavy aluminum foil, extending foil over ends of pan; lightly grease foil. Press dough into bottom of prepared pan. In a medium bowl, combine candied fruit and pecans. Sprinkle fruit mixture over dough; lightly press into dough. Bake 22 to 24 minutes or until edges are lightly browned. Lift from pan using ends of foil; allow to cool.

In a small saucepan, bring corn syrup to a boil. Boil 1 minute. Brush corn syrup over top of cookies; cool completely. Follow Cutting Diamond-Shaped Bars, page 122, to cut cookies. Store in an airtight container.

Yield: about 4 dozen cookies

PINEAPPLE JUMBLES

¹/₂	cup butter or margarine, softened
¹/₂	cup granulated sugar
¹/₂	cup firmly packed brown sugar
¹/₂	cup sour cream
1	egg
1	teaspoon vanilla extract
1¹/₄	cups all-purpose flour
¹/₄	teaspoon baking soda
¹/₄	teaspoon salt
1	cup sweetened shredded coconut
1	cup coarsely chopped walnuts
1	cup finely chopped candied pineapple

Preheat oven to 375 degrees. In a large bowl, cream butter and sugars until fluffy. Add sour cream, egg, and vanilla; beat un▪

...oth. In a small bowl, combine flour,
...ing soda, and salt. Add dry ingredients
...reamed mixture; stir until a soft dough
...ns. Stir in remaining ingredients. Drop
...espoonfuls of dough 2 inches apart onto
...eased baking sheet. Bake 10 to
...minutes or until edges are lightly
...wned. Transfer cookies to a wire rack to
...l. Store in an airtight container.

...d: about 4 dozen cookies

...STY CHRISTMAS WREATHS

...OKIES

¹/₃ cup butter or margarine,
       softened
¹/₃ cup firmly packed brown sugar
¹/₂ cup sifted confectioners sugar
 1   egg
 2   tablespoons grated lemon zest
¹/₂ teaspoon vanilla extract
¹/₄ cups all-purpose flour
¹/₄ cup cornstarch
¹/₂ teaspoon ground cardamom
¹/₄ teaspoon baking powder

...NG

 1   cup sifted confectioners sugar
 2   tablespoons milk

     Holly mix sprinkles to decorate

...or cookies, cream butter and sugars in
...rge bowl until fluffy. Add egg, lemon
..., and vanilla; beat until smooth. In a
...ll bowl, combine flour, cornstarch,
...damom, and baking powder. Add dry
...edients to creamed mixture; stir until a
...dough forms. Place dough on plastic
...p and shape into four 6-inch-long rolls.
...l 2 hours.

...reheat oven to 400 degrees. Cut each
...into 12 equal pieces. On a lightly
...red surface, roll each piece into a
...ch-long rope. Twist 2 ropes of dough
...ther. Place on a greased baking sheet.
...pe into wreaths and press ends together
...eal. Bake 6 to 8 minutes or until

Fun to make, these Tasty Christmas Wreaths are almost too pretty to eat! Fashioned from braided dough, the dainty cookies are embellished with a garland of icing and holly sprinkles.

bottoms are lightly browned. Transfer cookies to a wire rack with waxed paper underneath to cool.

For icing, combine confectioners sugar and milk; stir until smooth. Spoon icing into a pastry bag fitted with a small round tip. Pipe icing onto wreaths; place holly sprinkles on icing. Allow icing to harden. Store in an airtight container.

Yield: 2 dozen cookies

OLDIES BUT GOODIES

Generations of homemakers have indulged their loved ones with home-baked cookies, often sharing their favorite recipes with friends and family. Passed down through the years, these simple sweets were often reflective of the times and made with ingredients commonly found in the cupboard. This assortment of oldies but goodies includes the cookies you grew up with — Snickerdoodles, Old-fashioned Gingersnaps, and more. Some, like Mom's Sugar Cookies and Peanut Butter Bites, may have been the first ones you baked as a child. We hope these recipes will stir fond memories and inspire you to share them with your children, too.

(Previous page) *Always a tempting treat, Mom's Sugar Cookies (clockwise from left) are traditional favorites that will keep your family coming back to the cookie jar. Peanut Butter Bites are packed with nutty flavor to tantalize even the most finicky taste buds. Unusually delicious, Marguerites are simply saltine crackers topped with a fluffy meringue mixture.*

PEANUT BUTTER BITES

- $1/2$ cup butter or margarine, softened
- $1/2$ cup granulated sugar
- $1/2$ cup firmly packed brown sugar
- $3/4$ cup crunchy peanut butter
- 1 egg
- $1/2$ teaspoon vanilla extract
- $1^{1}/_3$ cups all-purpose flour
- $1/2$ teaspoon baking soda
- $1/2$ teaspoon baking powder
- $1/4$ teaspoon salt

Preheat oven to 375 degrees. In a large bowl, cream butter and sugars until fluffy. Add peanut butter, egg, and vanilla; beat until well blended. In a small bowl, combine flour, baking soda, baking powder, and salt. Add dry ingredients to creamed mixture; stir until a soft dough forms. Shape dough into balls slightly larger than $1/2$-inch and place 2 inches apart on an ungreased baking sheet. Flatten balls in a crisscross pattern with a fork dipped in flour. Bake 6 to 8 minutes or until bottoms are lightly browned. Transfer cookies to a wire rack to cool. Store in an airtight container.

Yield: about 8 dozen cookies

MARGUERITES

- 1 cup sugar
- $1/3$ cup water
- $1/8$ teaspoon salt
- 1 egg white
- $1/2$ cup finely chopped pecans
- 35 to 40 saltine crackers

In a heavy medium saucepan, combine sugar, water, and salt. Stirring constantly, cook over medium-low heat until sugar dissolves. Using a pastry brush dipped in hot water, wash down any sugar crystals on sides of pan. Attach a candy thermometer to pan, making sure thermometer does not touch bottom of pan. Increase heat to medium and bring to a boil. Cook, without stirring, until syrup reaches soft-ball stage (approximately 234 to 240 degrees). Test about $1/2$ teaspoon syrup in ice water. Syrup will easily form a ball in ice water but will flatten when held in your hand. Remove from heat. In a medium bowl, beat egg white until stiff. Beating constantly, slowly pour syrup over beaten egg white. Continue beating 1 to 2 minutes (mixture will be thick and glossy). Stir in pecans. Preheat oven to 325 degrees. Place crackers on an ungreased baking sheet. Spread a heaping tablespoonful of mixture on top of each cracker. Bake 8 to 10 minutes or until tops are set. Transfer cookies to a wire rack to cool. Store in an airtight container.

Yield: 35 to 40 cookies

MOM'S SUGAR COOKIES

- $3/4$ cup vegetable oil
- 2 eggs
- 2 teaspoons vanilla extract
- 1 cup sugar
- 2 cups all-purpose flour
- 1 teaspoon baking powder
- $1/4$ teaspoon salt
- Sugar

Preheat oven to 400 degrees. In a larg[e] bowl, beat oil, eggs, and vanilla until wel[l] blended. Add 1 cup sugar; beat until smooth. In a small bowl, combine flour, baking powder, and salt. Add dry ingredients to egg mixture; stir until a sof[t] dough forms. Drop teaspoonfuls of doug[h] 2 inches apart onto an ungreased baking sheet. Flatten cookies with bottom of a gl[ass] dipped in sugar. Bake 5 to 7 minutes or until bottoms are lightly browned. Transf[er] cookies to a wire rack to cool. Store in a cookie tin.

Yield: about 5 dozen cookies

BUTTERY PECAN COOKIES

- 1 cup butter or margarine, softened
- $2/3$ cup firmly packed brown sugar
- 1 teaspoon vanilla extract
- 2 cups all-purpose flour
- $3/4$ cup chopped pecans, toasted and coarsely ground
- $1/2$ teaspoon salt

In a medium bowl, cream butter, brow[n] sugar, and vanilla until fluffy. In a small bowl, combine flour, pecans, and salt. Ad[d] dry ingredients to creamed mixture; stir until a soft dough forms. Divide dough in[to] half; shape each half into an 8-inch-long roll. Wrap in plastic wrap and chill 1 hou[r].

Preheat oven to 350 degrees. Cut each roll into $1/4$-inch slices and place 1 inch apart on an ungreased baking sheet. Bak[e] 10 to 12 minutes or until edges are lightl[y] browned. Transfer cookies to a wire rac[k to] cool. Store in an airtight container.

Yield: about 4 dozen cookies

Cowboy Cookies (left) *corral three childhood favorites — chewy oats, chocolate chips, and pecans — in one tasty*
morsel! Bursting with crunchy goodness, Buttery Pecan Cookies are timeless treats.

COWBOY COOKIES

1 cup butter or margarine, melted
1 cup granulated sugar
1 cup firmly packed brown sugar
2 eggs
1 teaspoon vanilla extract
2 cups all-purpose flour
1 teaspoon baking powder
1 teaspoon baking soda
$^1/_2$ teaspoon salt

2 cups quick-cooking oats
1 package (12 ounces) semisweet
 chocolate chips
$^3/_4$ cup chopped pecans

Preheat oven to 350 degrees. In a large
bowl, beat butter and sugars until creamy.
Add eggs and vanilla; beat until smooth. In a
small bowl, combine flour, baking powder,
baking soda, and salt. Add dry ingredients

to creamed mixture; stir until a soft dough
forms. Stir in oats, chocolate chips, and
pecans. Drop tablespoonfuls of dough
2 inches apart onto a lightly greased baking
sheet. Bake 9 to 11 minutes or until edges
are lightly browned. Transfer cookies to a
wire rack to cool. Store in an airtight
container.

Yield: about 5$^1/_2$ dozen cookies

Spicy Hermits are chewy cookies that combine the traditional goodness of raisins and walnuts with rich coffee and molasses.

HERMITS

- 1 cup butter or margarine, softened
- 2 cups firmly packed brown sugar
- 2 eggs
- 1/4 cup molasses
- 1/4 cup strongly brewed coffee, cooled
- 1 teaspoon vanilla extract
- 3 cups all-purpose flour
- 1 teaspoon baking soda
- 1 teaspoon baking powder
- 1 teaspoon salt
- 1 teaspoon ground cinnamon
- 1/2 teaspoon ground allspice
- 1/4 teaspoon ground nutmeg
- 2 cups golden raisins, coarsely chopped
- 1 1/4 cups chopped walnuts

Preheat oven to 375 degrees. In a large bowl, cream butter and brown sugar until fluffy. Add eggs, molasses, coffee, and vanilla; beat until smooth. In a medium bowl, combine flour, baking soda, baking powder, salt, and spices. Add dry ingredients to creamed mixture; stir until a thick batter forms. Stir in raisins and walnuts. Drop tablespoonfuls of batter 2 inches apart onto a lightly greased baking sheet. Bake 7 to 9 minutes or until golden brown on tops. Transfer cookies to a wire rack to cool. Store in an airtight container

Yield: about 7 dozen cookies

LEMON WAFERS

- 1 cup butter or margarine, softened
- 3/4 cup sugar
- 1 egg
- 2 egg whites
- 1 tablespoon lemon extract
- 1 cup all-purpose flour

Preheat oven to 375 degrees. In a large bowl, cream butter and sugar until fluffy. Add egg, egg whites, and lemon extract; be

Big on taste, Lemon Wafers (left) *are little golden-edged sweets that melt in your mouth. Chocolate-Almond Dream rs present a rich, delicious filling of almonds, coconut, and chocolate chips spread over a buttery brown sugar crust.*

til smooth. Add flour to creamed mixture; r until a thick batter forms. Spoon batter o a pastry bag fitted with a large round . Pipe heaping teaspoonfuls of batter nches apart onto a baking sheet lined th parchment paper. Bake 5 to 7 minutes until edges are lightly browned. Transfer okies to a wire rack to cool. Store in an rtight container.

eld: about 7 dozen cookies

HOCOLATE-ALMOND REAM BARS

RUST

1 cup all-purpose flour
1/2 cup butter or margarine, softened
1/2 cup firmly packed brown sugar

FILLING

1 1/4 cups sliced almonds, toasted
1 cup sweetened shredded coconut
3/4 cup semisweet chocolate chips
2 tablespoons all-purpose flour
3/4 teaspoon baking powder
1/4 teaspoon salt
3/4 cup firmly packed brown sugar
2 eggs
1 1/2 teaspoons vanilla extract

Preheat oven to 350 degrees. For crust, mix flour, butter, and brown sugar in a medium bowl with a fork until well blended. Line a 9 x 13-inch baking pan with aluminum foil, extending foil over ends of pan. Press crust into bottom of prepared pan. Bake 10 minutes.

For filling, combine almonds, coconut, chocolate chips, flour, baking powder, and salt in a medium bowl. In a small bowl, beat brown sugar, eggs, and vanilla until well blended. Add to dry ingredients; stir until well blended. Spoon over hot crust. Bake 15 to 20 minutes or until center is set and lightly browned on top. Cool in pan 10 minutes. Cut into 1 x 2-inch bars while warm; cool completely. Store in an airtight container.

Yield: about 4 dozen bars

Rolled in cinnamon and sugar before they're baked, Snickerdoodles are sweet treats that you can make up in a jiffy with ingredients on hand. A heart-shaped cookie jar tag says your cookies are baked with love!

SNICKERDOODLES

    1   cup butter or margarine, softened
 1^1/$_2$ cups sugar, divided
    2   eggs
    1   teaspoon vanilla extract
 2^1/$_2$ cups all-purpose flour
 1^1/$_2$ teaspoons ground cinnamon,
          divided
    1   teaspoon cream of tartar
    1   teaspoon baking soda
 ^{1}/$_4$ teaspoon salt

Preheat oven to 375 degrees. In a large bowl, cream butter and 1^1/$_4$ cups sugar until fluffy. Add eggs and vanilla; beat until smooth. In a medium bowl, combine flour, ^{1}/$_2$ teaspoon cinnamon, cream of tartar, baking soda, and salt. Add dry ingredients to creamed mixture; stir until a soft dough forms. In a small bowl, combine remaining ^{1}/$_4$ cup sugar and 1 teaspoon cinnamon. Shape dough into 1-inch balls and roll in sugar mixture. Place balls 2 inches apart a lightly greased baking sheet. Bake 6 to 8 minutes or until bottoms are lightly browned. Transfer cookies to a wire rack cool. Store in an airtight container.

Yield: about 7 dozen cookies

OLD-FASHIONED GINGERSNAPS

 1^1/$_2$ cups butter or margarine, softened
 2^3/$_4$ cups sugar, divided
    2   eggs
 ^{1}/$_2$ cup molasses
    4   cups all-purpose flour
    2   teaspoons baking soda
    2   teaspoons ground cinnamon
    2   teaspoons ground cloves
    2   teaspoons ground ginger
        Sugar

Preheat oven to 375 degrees. In a large bowl, cream butter and 2 cups sugar until fluffy. Add eggs and molasses; beat until smooth. In a medium bowl, combine flour, baking soda, cinnamon, cloves, and ginger. Add dry ingredients to creamed mixture; stir until a soft dough forms. Shape dough into 1-inch balls and roll in remaining ^{3}/$_4$ cup sugar. Place balls 3 inches apart on a lightly greased baking sheet; flatten with bottom a glass dipped in sugar. Bake 5 to 7 minutes or until bottoms are lightly browned. Transfer cookies to a wire rack to cool. Store in an airtight container.

Yield: about 10 dozen cookies

The taste of Oatmeal Family Favorites (top) and Old-fashioned Gingersnaps will bring to mind afternoons spent visiting Grandmother's house. The oatmeal cookies are just as good as you remember, and the gingersnaps are thin and chewy. Add to the nostalgia by serving these sweets in Shaker boxes decorated with homespun fabric and buttons.

OATMEAL FAMILY FAVORITES

1³/4 cups granulated sugar, divided
1 cup firmly packed brown sugar
1 cup vegetable oil
3 eggs
1 teaspoon vanilla extract
1 cup all-purpose flour
1 teaspoon baking soda
¹/2 teaspoon salt
4 cups quick-cooking oats
1 cup sweetened shredded coconut
Granulated sugar

Preheat oven to 350 degrees. In a large bowl, combine 1 cup granulated sugar, brown sugar, and oil; beat until well blended. Add eggs and vanilla; beat until smooth. In a small bowl, combine flour, baking soda, and salt. Add dry ingredients to sugar mixture; stir until a soft dough forms. Stir in oats and coconut until well blended. Shape dough into 1-inch balls and roll in remaining ³/4 cup granulated sugar. Place balls 2 inches apart on a greased baking sheet; flatten with bottom of a glass dipped in granulated sugar. Bake 8 to 10 minutes or until edges are lightly browned. Cool cookies on pan 3 minutes; transfer to a wire rack to cool completely. Store in an airtight container.

Yield: about 8 dozen cookies

KID PLEASERS

If there were a fantasyland for children, it would be filled with ice cream, peanut butter, and every form of chocolate imaginable! Like a dream come true, this collection of cute and tasty cookies is sure to tickle a youngster's taste buds. Kids will be enchanted by the bubble gum-flavored "ice-cream cones" and the novelty root beer-flavored cookies that are shaped and decorated like frosty floats. They can even join in the fun of making easy no-bake chocolate stars and chewy coconut-dipped "monsters." These fairy-tale confections are perfect for birthday parties, celebrations, sleep overs, or rainy day activities!

No-Bake Chocolate Stars	Root Beer Floats
Chocolate Malted Cookies	Soccer Ball Cookies
Ice-Cream Cone Cookies	Candy Bar Pizzas
Peanut Butter and Jelly Creams	Butterscotch Chewies
Hairy Monsters	United States Maps

(Previous page) *Chewy Chocolate Malted Cookies* (from top left) *are reminiscent of a soda-fountain favorite. Bubble gum-flavored icing and confetti sprinkles top our Ice-Cream Cone Cookies. No-Bake Chocolate Stars are extra-easy to make using crispy cocoa-flavored rice cereal and peanut butter.*

NO-BAKE CHOCOLATE STARS

- 1 cup sugar
- 1 cup light corn syrup
- 1 cup smooth peanut butter
- 6 cups cocoa-flavored crispy rice cereal

In a heavy medium saucepan, combine sugar and corn syrup over medium-high heat; stir frequently until mixture boils. Allow to boil 30 seconds without stirring. Remove from heat and stir in peanut butter. Place cereal in a large bowl. Pour peanut butter mixture over cereal; stir until well blended. With well-greased hands, press mixture into a greased 4 1/2-inch-wide by 1-inch-deep star-shaped mold. Immediately remove from mold; transfer to a lightly greased sheet of aluminum foil to cool. Repeat with remaining cereal, working quickly before mixture cools. Store in an airtight container.

Yield: about 14 stars

CHOCOLATE MALTED COOKIES

- 2 cups granulated sugar
- 6 ounces semisweet baking chocolate, melted
- 1/4 cup butter or margarine, melted
- 4 eggs
- 2 cups all-purpose flour
- 2 teaspoons baking powder
- 1/2 teaspoon salt

- 1 cup malted milk crunch, divided (used in candy making)
- 3/4 cup sifted confectioners sugar

Combine sugar, melted chocolate, and melted butter in a large bowl. Add eggs, 1 at a time, beating well after each addition. In a small bowl, combine flour, baking powder, and salt. Add dry ingredients to chocolate mixture; stir until a soft dough forms. Stir in 3/4 cup malted milk crunch. Cover dough and chill 1 hour.

Preheat oven to 300 degrees. Shape dough into 1-inch balls. In a small bowl, combine remaining 1/4 cup malted milk crunch and confectioners sugar. Roll balls in confectioners sugar mixture and place 2 inches apart on a baking sheet lined with parchment paper. Bake 10 to 12 minutes or until tops are cracked. Cool cookies on pan 3 minutes; transfer to a wire rack to cool completely. Store in an airtight container.

Yield: about 6 1/2 dozen cookies

ICE-CREAM CONE COOKIES

COOKIES

- 1 can (8 ounces) almond paste, coarsely crumbled
- 3/4 cup butter or margarine, softened
- 1/2 cup granulated sugar
- 1/2 cup sifted confectioners sugar
- 1 egg
- 1/2 teaspoon vanilla extract
- 1/8 teaspoon bubble gum-flavored oil (used in candy making)
- 2 1/4 cups all-purpose flour

ICING

- 2 cups sifted confectioners sugar
- 3 tablespoons milk
- 10 drops bubble gum-flavored oil (used in candy making)
  Pink paste food coloring
  Pastel confetti sprinkles to decorate

For cookies, place almond paste in a large microwave-safe bowl. Microwave on high power (100%) 25 seconds to soften. Add butter and sugars to almond paste; cream until fluffy. Add egg, vanilla, and flavored oil; beat until smooth. Gradually add flour; stir until a soft dough forms. Divide dough into thirds. Wrap in plastic wrap and chill 1 hour.

Preheat oven to 350 degrees. On a lightly floured surface, use a floured rolling pin to roll out one third of dough to 1/4-inch thickness. Use a 2 1/2 x 3 3/4-inch ice-cream cone-shaped cookie cutter to cut out cookies. Transfer to a lightly greased baking sheet. Bake 7 to 9 minutes or until bottoms are lightly browned. Transfer cookies to a wire rack with waxed paper underneath to cool. Repeat with remaining dough.

For icing, combine confectioners sugar, milk, and flavored oil in a medium bowl; stir until smooth. Tint pink. Ice tops of cookies to resemble ice cream. Sprinkle icing with confetti sprinkles before icing hardens. Allow icing to harden. Store in an airtight container.

Yield: about 4 dozen cookies

PEANUT BUTTER AND JELLY CREAMS

COOKIES

- 3/4 cup butter or margarine, softened
- 1/2 cup smooth peanut butter
- 1/2 cup granulated sugar
- 1/2 cup firmly packed brown sugar
- 1 egg
- 1 1/4 cups all-purpose flour
- 1 teaspoon baking powder
- 1/4 teaspoon salt

FILLING

- 1 3/4 cups sifted confectioners sugar
- 1/4 cup butter or margarine, softened
- 4 teaspoons whipping cream
- 4 teaspoons raspberry jelly
  Pink paste food coloring

or cookies, cream butter, peanut butter,
rs, and egg until fluffy. In a small bowl,
bine dry ingredients; add to creamed
ture. Stir until a soft dough forms. Cover
gh and chill 2 hours.

reheat oven to 350 degrees. Divide
led dough into fourths. On a heavily
red surface, use a floured rolling pin to
out one fourth of dough at a time to
nch thickness. Use a 3-inch-wide star-
ped cookie cutter to cut out cookies.
sfer to an ungreased baking sheet.
e 7 to 9 minutes or until bottoms are
ly browned. Transfer cookies to a wire
k to cool.

or filling, combine first 4 ingredients in
nall bowl. Tint pink. Spread about
aspoons of filling between 2 cookies.
eat with remaining filling and cookies.
e in an airtight container.

d: about 2 dozen cookies

IRY MONSTERS

2 cup butter or margarine
4 cup sugar
1 egg
1 cup chopped dates
2 cups fruit-flavored crispy rice
    cereal
1 cup salted peanuts, coarsely
    chopped
1 teaspoon vanilla extract
3 cups finely shredded sweetened
    coconut

Whisking constantly, combine butter,
ar, and egg in a heavy medium skillet
r medium heat. Add dates to butter
ture. Continue to cook and whisk
ture about 10 minutes, mashing as dates
en. Remove from heat; stir in cereal,
nuts, and vanilla. When mixture is cool
ugh to handle, use greased hands to
pe into 1-inch balls; roll in coconut.
l. Store in an airtight container.

d: about 4 dozen cookies

Packed with peanuts and rolled in shredded coconut, Hairy Monsters
(in bowl) *will have kids screaming for more. A sweet raspberry filling
is sandwiched between star-shaped cookies for our Peanut Butter and
Jelly Creams.*

Cut from a mug pattern, our "frothy" Root Beer Floats are decorated with piped-on icing. Root beer-flavored oil gives these soft and chewy cookies their distinctive flavor.

ROOT BEER FLOATS

COOKIES

- 1 cup butter or margarine, softened
- 1¹/₂ cups sifted confectioners sugar
- 1 egg
- 1 teaspoon vanilla extract
- ¹/₄ teaspoon root beer-flavored oil (used in candy making)
- 2¹/₂ cups all-purpose flour
- ¹/₂ teaspoon baking soda
- ¹/₄ teaspoon cream of tartar

ICING

- 1¹/₂ cups sifted confectioners sugar
- 3 tablespoons butter or margarine, softened
- ¹/₄ teaspoon root beer-flavored oil (used in candy making)
- 1¹/₂ tablespoons milk
  Brown paste food coloring
- 2 tubes (4.25 ounces each) purchased white decorating icing

Note: Use pattern, page 118, and follow Cutting Out Cookies, page 122.

For cookies, cream butter and confectioners sugar in a large bowl until fluffy. Add egg, vanilla, and flavored oil; beat until smooth. In a medium bowl, combine flour, baking soda, and cream of tartar. Add dry ingredients to creamed mixture; stir until a soft dough forms. Divide dough in half. Wrap in plastic wrap and chill 3 hours.

Preheat oven to 375 degrees. On a lightly floured surface, use a floured rolling pin to roll out half of dough to ¹/₈-inch thickness. Cut out cookies. Transfer cookies to a lightly greased baking sheet. Bake 5 to 7 minutes or until bottoms are lightly browned. Transfer to a wire rack to cool. Repeat with remaining dough.

For icing, combine confectioners sugar, butter, flavored oil, and milk in a medium bowl; stir until smooth. Tint brown. Spoon brown icing into a pastry bag fitted with a small round tip. Pipe outline of mug onto cookies. Allow icing to harden. Use white decorating icing directly from tube to pipe root beer "foam" onto tops of cookies. Allow icing to harden. Store in single layer between sheets of waxed paper in an airtight container.

Yield: about 5¹/₂ dozen cookies

SOCCER BALL COOKIES

COOKIES

3/4 cup butter or margarine, softened
1 cup granulated sugar
1 cup firmly packed brown sugar
1/2 cup smooth peanut butter
1 egg
1 teaspoon vanilla extract
3 cups all-purpose flour
1/2 teaspoon baking powder
1/2 teaspoon baking soda
1/4 teaspoon salt

WHITE ICING

5 cups sifted confectioners sugar
6 tablespoons plus 1/2 teaspoon to
    2 teaspoons milk
1 teaspoon clear vanilla extract
    (used in cake decorating)

BLACK ICING

1/2 cups sifted confectioners sugar
1 tablespoon black powdered food
    coloring
3 tablespoons plus 1/2 teaspoon
    milk, divided
1/2 teaspoon vanilla extract

Trace patterns (including heavy lines), page 119, onto white paper; cut out center and 5 side pieces. Preheat oven to 0 degrees. For cookies, cream butter and sugars in a large bowl until fluffy. Add peanut butter, egg, and vanilla; beat until smooth. In a medium bowl, combine flour, baking powder, baking soda, and salt. Add ingredients to creamed mixture; stir until well blended. Spread dough into greased 12-inch-diameter pizza pans. Bake 15 to 17 minutes or until tops are lightly browned. Cool cookies in pans minutes. Invert cookies onto serving plates and cool completely.

For white icing, combine confectioners sugar, 6 tablespoons milk, and vanilla in a medium bowl; stir until smooth. Add additional milk, 1/2 teaspoon at a time, for

Kids are sure to get a kick out of these giant peanut-buttery cookies decorated to resemble soccer balls. To celebrate the end of the season or a big win, share the generously sized Soccer Ball Cookies with your child's fellow teammates. These treats are sure to score!

desired consistency. Ice cookies. Allow icing to harden. Place center pattern piece in center of 1 cookie. Matching heavy lines, place side pattern pieces on cookie next to center piece. Using the end of a toothpick, mark each corner of pattern pieces. Remove patterns. Repeat for remaining cookie.

For black icing, combine confectioners sugar, food coloring, 3 tablespoons milk, and vanilla in a small bowl; stir until smooth. Spoon 1/3 cup icing into a pastry bag fitted with a small round tip. Using holes as a guide, pipe lines between holes onto both cookies, extending lines down sides as necessary. Place remaining icing in a small bowl; add remaining 1/2 teaspoon milk. Ice areas as shown in photo. Allow icing to harden. If desired, use icing in pastry bag to pipe team and/or member names onto cookies. Store in an airtight container.

Yield: two 12-inch cookies, 12 servings each

Chewy, gooey Candy Bar Pizzas (left) are chock-full of peanuts, chocolate, and caramel for a fantastically rich treat. The oatmeal crust, made with brown sugar and peanut butter, is a tasty sweet all by itself! Loaded with butterscotch chips and pecans, these delightful Butterscotch Chewies live up to their tempting name.

CANDY BAR PIZZAS

CRUST

- 2 cups quick-cooking oats
- 1/2 cup firmly packed brown sugar
- 1/3 cup light corn syrup
- 2 tablespoons butter or margarine, melted
- 2 tablespoons chunky peanut butter
- 1/2 teaspoon vanilla extract

FILLING

- 26 caramels (about 1/2 of a 14-ounce package)
- 2 tablespoons water
- 1 package (6 ounces) semisweet chocolate chips
- 1/3 cup chunky peanut butter
- 2 teaspoons vegetable shortening
- 1/2 cup salted peanuts

Preheat oven to 350 degrees. For crust, combine oats, brown sugar, and corn syrup in a large bowl. Add melted butter, peanut butter, and vanilla; stir until well blended. Press mixture into bottoms of two 9-inch round cake pans. Bake 10 to 12 minutes or until lightly browned. Cool in pans 10 minutes.

For filling, microwave caramels and water in a medium microwave-safe bowl on high power (100%) 2 minutes, stirring after 1 minute. Spread evenly over crusts. Microwave chocolate chips in a medium microwave-safe bowl on medium-high power (80%) 2 minutes, stirring after 1 minute. Add peanut butter and shortening; stir until well blended. Stir in peanuts.

Spread filling over caramel layers. Chill 30 minutes or until chocolate is firm. Cut into wedges to serve.

Yield: two 9-inch pizzas, 16 servings each

BUTTERSCOTCH CHEWIES

- 2/3 cup butter or margarine, softened
- 1 1/2 cups firmly packed brown sugar
- 2 eggs
- 1 teaspoon vanilla extract
- 1 1/2 cups all-purpose flour
- 1/4 teaspoon baking soda
- 1 package (10 or 12 ounces) butterscotch chips
- 1 cup chopped pecans

reheat oven to 375 degrees. In a large
l, cream butter and brown sugar until
. Add eggs and vanilla; beat until
oth. In a medium bowl, combine flour
baking soda. Add dry ingredients to
med mixture; stir until a soft dough
s. Stir in butterscotch chips and
ns. Drop tablespoonfuls of dough
ches apart onto a greased baking sheet.
e 7 to 9 minutes or until bottoms are
ly browned. Transfer cookies to a wire
 to cool. Store in single layers between
ts of waxed paper in an airtight
ainer.

l: about 4 dozen cookies

ITED STATES MAPS

 cup butter or margarine, softened
 cup sifted confectioners sugar
 cup firmly packed brown sugar
 egg
 teaspoon maple flavoring
 cups all-purpose flour
 teaspoon salt
 Star-shaped sprinkles

 a large bowl, cream butter and sugars
 fluffy. Add egg and maple flavoring;
 until smooth. In a small bowl, combine
 r and salt. Add dry ingredients to
med mixture; stir until a soft dough
s. Divide dough in half. Wrap in plastic
 and chill 1 hour.
reheat oven to 350 degrees. On a lightly
ed surface, use a floured rolling pin to
out half of dough to 1/4-inch thickness.
 a 3 x 2-inch United States-shaped
kie cutter to cut out cookies. Transfer to
eased baking sheet. Place star-shaped
nkles on cookies to represent different
s. Bake 6 to 8 minutes or until bottoms
s. lightly browned. Transfer cookies to a
 rack to cool. Repeat with remaining
gh. Store in an airtight container.

l: about 3 dozen cookies

*These maple-flavored United States Maps are a neat — and yummy —
teaching tool! Give your little helpers a quick lesson in U.S. geography by
having them mark their home state with a star-shaped candy sprinkle.*

SPECIAL OCCASIONS

When the celebration calls for treats as special as the occasion, you'll want to create confections like our bow-tied bears for a baby shower or apple-shaped marzipan cookies for taking to teacher on the first day of school. This sampling offers something sweet for many of life's milestones, including birthdays, weddings, and even graduation day! Whatever the reason, make the day even more memorable with these delectable delights.

Almond Delights	Almond Cookie Tree
Birthday Party Cookies	Wedding Bells
Cashew Dreams	Marzipan Apple Cookies
Baby Bears	Graduation Day Cookies

(Previous page) *Kids will really go for soft and chewy Birthday Party Cookies* (from left). *The star-shaped sweets are topped with icing and colorful non-pareils. The nutty appeal of Cashew Dreams will have you wistfully wishing for more. The shortbread cookies are made with just a few simple ingredients. Chocolate-covered almonds are placed in the centers of our rich Almond Delights while they're still warm from the oven.*

ALMOND DELIGHTS

1 cup butter or margarine, softened
1 package (3 ounces) cream cheese, softened
1 cup sugar
1 egg yolk
1 teaspoon almond extract
2 1/2 cups all-purpose flour
3 packages (2.8 ounces each) chocolate-covered whole almonds (about 1 cup)

In a large bowl, cream butter, cream cheese, and sugar until fluffy. Add egg yolk and almond extract; beat until smooth. Add flour to creamed mixture; stir until a soft dough forms. Wrap in plastic wrap and chill 1 hour.

Preheat oven to 325 degrees. Shape dough into 1-inch balls and place 2 inches apart on a greased baking sheet. Use thumb to make a slight indentation in top of each ball. Bake 12 to 15 minutes or until bottoms are lightly browned. Press 1 almond into center of each warm cookie. Transfer cookies to a wire rack to cool. Store in an airtight container.

Yield: about 6 dozen cookies

BIRTHDAY PARTY COOKIES

COOKIES

3/4 cup butter or margarine, softened
1/2 cup granulated sugar
1/2 cup sifted confectioners sugar
1 egg
2 teaspoons vanilla extract
1 teaspoon butter flavoring
2 1/4 cups all-purpose flour
2 tablespoons cornstarch
1/4 teaspoon salt

ICING

2 cups sifted confectioners sugar
3 tablespoons plus 1 teaspoon milk, divided
1/2 teaspoon clear vanilla extract (used in cake decorating)
    Multicolored non-pareils to decorate

For cookies, cream butter and sugars in a large bowl until fluffy. Add egg, vanilla, and butter flavoring; beat until smooth. In a medium bowl, combine flour, cornstarch, and salt. Add dry ingredients to creamed mixture; stir until a soft dough forms. Divide dough in half. Wrap in plastic wrap and chill 2 hours.

Preheat oven to 350 degrees. On a lightly floured surface, use a floured rolling pin to roll out half of dough to 1/4-inch thickness. Use a 3-inch star-shaped cookie cutter to cut out cookies. Place 2 inches apart on a greased baking sheet. Bake 8 to 10 minutes or until bottoms are lightly browned. Transfer cookies to a wire rack to cool. Repeat with remaining dough.

For icing, combine confectioners sugar, 2 tablespoons plus 2 teaspoons milk, and vanilla in a small bowl; stir until smooth. Place 1/2 cup icing in another small bowl and add remaining 2 teaspoons milk to thin; cover and set aside. Spoon remaining icing into a pastry bag fitted with a small round tip. Pipe outline onto each cookie. Allow

icing to harden. Using a small paintbrush, paint reserved thinned icing inside piped lines on tops of cookies. Sprinkle non-pareils over cookies before icing hardens. Allow icing to harden. Store in an airtight container.

Yield: about 3 1/2 dozen cookies

CASHEW DREAMS

COOKIES

1 cup butter or margarine, softened
6 tablespoons sugar
1 teaspoon vanilla extract
2 cups all-purpose flour
1 1/2 cups coarsely chopped lightly salted cashews

ICING

1 1/4 cups sifted confectioners sugar
1 1/2 to 2 tablespoons milk
1/2 teaspoon vanilla extract

Preheat oven to 325 degrees. For cookies, cream butter, sugar, and vanilla a medium bowl until fluffy. Add flour; stir until a soft dough forms. Stir in cashews. Shape dough into 1-inch balls and place 2 inches apart on a greased baking sheet. Slightly flatten balls with fingers. Bake 8 to 10 minutes or until bottoms are lightly browned. Transfer cookies to a wire rack to cool.

For icing, combine confectioners sugar, 1 1/2 tablespoons milk, and vanilla in a small bowl; stir until smooth, adding additional milk as necessary, 1/2 teaspoon at a time, to spread easily. Ice cookies. Allow icing to harden. Store in an airtight container.

Yield: about 4 dozen cookies

BABY BEARS

COOKIES

- ¹/₂ cup butter or margarine, softened
- ¹/₂ cup granulated sugar
- ¹/₂ cup firmly packed brown sugar
- 1 egg
- ¹/₂ teaspoon vanilla extract
- 1¹/₂ cups all-purpose flour
- ¹/₂ teaspoon baking powder
- ¹/₂ teaspoon ground cinnamon
- ¹/₄ teaspoon salt

ICING

- 2 cups sifted confectioners sugar
- 4 tablespoons vegetable shortening
- ¹/₂ teaspoon clear vanilla extract
  (used in cake decorating)
- 2¹/₂ to 3 tablespoons milk
  Blue and pink paste food coloring

For cookies, cream butter and sugars in large bowl until fluffy. Add egg and vanilla; beat until smooth. In a small bowl, combine flour, baking powder, cinnamon, and salt. Add dry ingredients to creamed mixture; stir until a soft dough forms. Divide dough in half. Wrap in plastic wrap and chill 2 hours.

Preheat oven to 375 degrees. On a lightly floured surface, use a floured rolling pin to roll out dough to ¹/₈-inch thickness. Use a 1¹/₄ x 1¹/₂-inch bear-shaped cookie cutter to cut out cookies. Transfer to an ungreased baking sheet. Bake 8 to 10 minutes or until edges are lightly browned. Transfer cookies to a wire rack to cool.

For icing, combine confectioners sugar, shortening, vanilla, and 2¹/₂ tablespoons milk in a small bowl; stir until smooth, adding additional milk for desired consistency. Spoon ¹/₂ cup icing each into small bowls. Tint blue and pink. Spoon blue, pink, and remaining white icing into pastry bags fitted with small round tips. Pipe white diaper and a pink hair bow or a blue bow tie on each cookie. Allow icing to harden. Store in an airtight container.

Yield: about 10 dozen cookies

The honored mother-to-be will love our cute Baby Bears, which are decorated with little white icing diapers and pink hair bows for girls or blue bow ties for boys. Dressed up with a bib and other baby essentials, a glass container is filled with these soft and cinnamony teddies for a sweet presentation.

Ring-shaped cookies in graduated sizes are simply stacked to create this pretty Almond Cookie Tree. A unique and welcome addition to traditional bridal shower fare, this scrumptious confection is embellished with tiny candied violets and loops of icing. Top it with a lovely bow in the bride's wedding colors.

ALMOND COOKIE TREE

COOKIES

1 can (8 ounces) almond paste, coarsely crumbled
1 cup butter or margarine, softened
1¼ cups sifted confectioners sugar
2 eggs
1 teaspoon almond extract
½ teaspoon vanilla extract
2 cups all-purpose flour
¾ cup cornstarch

ICING

1 cup sifted confectioners sugar
4½ teaspoons milk
⅛ teaspoon almond extract

Candied violets and violet paste food coloring to decorate

Preheat oven to 350 degrees. For cookies, use a black pen and patterns, page 120, to trace circles about 3 inches apart onto sheets of parchment paper. Pla almond paste in a large microwave-safe bowl. Microwave on high power (100%) 25 seconds to soften. Add butter and beat with an electric mixer until smooth. Add confectioners sugar and beat until fluffy. Add eggs and extracts; beat until smooth. In a small bowl, combine flour and cornstarch. Gradually add dry ingredients creamed mixture; stir until a very soft doug forms. Spoon dough into a pastry bag fitted with a very large round tip (#1A). Turn parchment paper over, with lines facing down, on a baking sheet and pipe dough around outside edges of circles. To reinforce each of the 3 largest circles, pipe a second circle of dough just inside and touching first dough circle. Bake 12 to 14 minutes or until bottoms are lightly browned. Transfer cookies to a wire rack with waxed paper underneath to cool.

For icing, combine all ingredients in a small bowl; stir until smooth. Spoon icing into a pastry bag fitted with a small round

. Pipe loops of icing onto each cookie.
ow icing to harden. To stack cookies,
e a ring of icing onto a serving plate and
ce largest cookie on icing. Stack
maining cookies from largest to smallest.
e a small amount of icing to place
ndied violets on cookies. Tint remaining
ng violet and spoon into a pastry bag
ed with a small round tip. Pipe centers
to violet flowers. Store in an airtight
ntainer.

eld: one 7¹⁄₂-inch-high cookie tree

EDDING BELLS

OKIES

1 cup butter or margarine, softened
1 cup granulated sugar
¹⁄₂ cup sifted confectioners sugar
1 egg
1 teaspoon almond extract
¹⁄₂ cups all-purpose flour
¹⁄₂ teaspoon baking powder
¹⁄₄ teaspoon salt

NG

¹⁄₄ cup water
1 tablespoon light corn syrup
3 cups plus 3 tablespoons sifted
    confectioners sugar
¹⁄₂ teaspoon almond extract
    Silver dragées to decorate

Preheat oven to 375 degrees. For
okies, cream butter and sugars in a large
wl until fluffy. Add egg and almond
tract; beat until smooth. In a medium
wl, combine flour, baking powder, and
lt. Add dry ingredients to creamed
ixture; stir until a soft dough forms. On a
htly floured surface, use a floured rolling
n to roll out dough to ¹⁄₄-inch thickness.
e a 2¹⁄₂ x 3-inch bell-shaped cookie
tter to cut out cookies. Place 2 inches
art on a greased baking sheet. Use end
a drinking straw to cut holes in tops of
okies. Bake 7 to 9 minutes or until

*Arranged on silvery doilies along with the place cards, Wedding Bells are
elegant tidbits to nibble at a wedding rehearsal dinner or formal reception. The
sugar cookie cutouts are topped with almond-flavored icing and silver dragées.*

bottoms are lightly browned. Transfer
cookies to a wire rack with waxed paper
underneath to cool.

For icing, combine water and corn syrup
in a heavy medium saucepan. Add
confectioners sugar and stir until well
blended. Attach a candy thermometer to
pan, making sure thermometer does not
touch bottom of pan. Stirring constantly,

cook over medium-low heat until icing
reaches 100 degrees. Remove from heat;
stir in almond extract. Cool icing 5 minutes.
Stirring icing occasionally, ice cookies.
Decorate cookies with dragées before icing
hardens. Allow icing to harden. Store in an
airtight container.

Yield: about 4¹⁄₂ dozen cookies

Ideal treats for a teacher on the first day of school, Marzipan Apple Cookies have a rich almond taste. Tinted with food coloring, the "apples" feature cloves as clever stems and slivers of green gumdrops for the leaves. These soft cookies will receive an A⁺ for creativity!

MARZIPAN APPLE COOKIES

1 can (8 ounces) almond paste, coarsely crumbled
1 cup butter, softened
¼ cup sugar
1 egg
1 teaspoon vanilla extract
2½ cups all-purpose flour
⅛ teaspoon salt
   Red paste food coloring
   Whole cloves and green gumdrops

Place almond paste in a large microwave-safe bowl. Microwave on high power (100%) 25 seconds to soften. Add butter and beat with an electric mixer until smooth. Add sugar and beat until fluffy. Add egg and vanilla; beat until smooth. Add flour and salt to creamed mixture; stir until a soft dough forms. Tint red. Divide dough in half. Cover dough and chill 1 hour.

Preheat oven to 350 degrees. Shape heaping teaspoonfuls of dough into about 1¼-inch balls. Use thumb to make a small indentation in top of each ball. Insert a whole clove and a small sliver of gumdrop into indentation for stem and leaf. Bake 9 to 11 minutes or until bottoms are lightly browned. Transfer cookies to a wire rack cool. Store in single layers between sheets of waxed paper in an airtight container.

Yield: about 5 dozen cookies

74

A creamy white chocolate filling is piped into rolled wafers for our Graduation Day Cookies. Tied with ribbons in your favorite graduates' school colors, the novel treats are a great way to celebrate their scholarly success.

GRADUATION DAY COOKIES

¹/₂ cup butter or margarine, softened
¹/₂ cup sugar
¹/₂ cup all-purpose flour
 2 egg whites
 1 teaspoon almond extract
 6 ounces white chocolate
 1 teaspoon vegetable shortening
   Narrow ribbons in school colors
     to decorate

Preheat oven to 400 degrees. In a medium bowl, cream butter and sugar until fluffy. Stir in flour. In a small bowl, beat egg whites until foamy. Beat egg whites and almond extract into dough. Making 4 to 6 cookies at a time, drop teaspoonfuls of dough 4 inches apart onto a baking sheet lined with parchment paper. Spread dough slightly with the back of a spoon. Bake 5 to 6 minutes or until edges are lightly browned. Roll each warm cookie around handle of a small wooden spoon. Transfer cookies to a wire rack, seam side down, to cool.

Stirring constantly, melt chocolate over low heat in a small saucepan. Remove from heat. Stir in shortening; allow mixture to cool slightly. Spoon chocolate mixture into a pastry bag fitted with a small round tip. Pipe chocolate into cookie rolls; allow chocolate to harden. Tie ribbons around cookies. Store in an airtight container.

Yield: about 3¹/₂ dozen cookies

SOPHISTICATED TASTES

Whether it's an open house, a reception, or an elegant evening affair, our gourmet confections will delight guests with discriminating tastes! This sweet assortment is laced with rich liqueurs and scrumptious nuts to please adult palates. Ornate serving trays laden with these delicious tidbits, a table set with an exquisite tea service, and intricate vases filled with roses will add all the splendor your special occasion deserves.

Chocolate-Almond Macaroons	Anise Seed Biscotti
Pistachio Swirls	Chocolate-Nut Truffle Cookies
Pecan-Praline Bars	Palmiers
Spiced Fruit Ravioli Cookies	Black Forest Brownies
Amaretto Florentines	Raspberry-Almond Bars
Orange Cappuccino Cookies	Chocolate Addictions

(Previous page) *Chewy coconut and crunchy almonds add to the decadent fudge flavor of Chocolate-Almond Macaroons (from left). Sliced Pistachio Swirls will brighten the dessert tray with colorful pistachios rolled into a lemon-flavored dough. A flaky crust is topped with a mixture of toasted pecans and a nutty liqueur to create Pecan-Praline Bars.*

CHOCOLATE-ALMOND MACAROONS

    3 tablespoons butter or margarine
 1/2 cup cocoa
    1 can (14 ounces) sweetened
        condensed milk
    2 teaspoons vanilla extract
 1/8 teaspoon salt
    1 package (14 ounces) sweetened
        shredded coconut
 1 1/2 cups sliced almonds, toasted and
        coarsely chopped

Preheat oven to 350 degrees. Place butter in a medium microwave-safe bowl. Microwave on medium-high power (80%) 1 minute or until butter is melted. Stir cocoa into melted butter. Add sweetened condensed milk, vanilla, and salt; stir until well blended. Place coconut in a large bowl; pour cocoa mixture over coconut and stir until well blended. Stir in almonds. Shape 1/2 tablespoonfuls of mixture into balls and place on a baking sheet lined with parchment paper. Bake 7 to 9 minutes or until edges are lightly browned. Transfer cookies to a wire rack to cool. Store in an airtight container.

Yield: about 7 dozen cookies

PISTACHIO SWIRLS

 3/4 cup butter or margarine, softened
 1/2 cup sugar
    1 egg
    1 tablespoon lemon juice
 1/2 teaspoon lemon zest
 1/2 teaspoon vanilla extract
 1 3/4 cups all-purpose flour
 1/4 teaspoon salt
 1 1/4 cups finely chopped pistachio nuts
 1/4 cup honey

In a large bowl, cream butter and sugar until fluffy. Add egg, lemon juice, lemon zest, and vanilla; beat until smooth. In a small bowl, combine flour and salt. Add dry ingredients to creamed mixture; stir until a soft dough forms. Divide dough in half. Wrap in plastic wrap and chill 2 hours or until dough is firm enough to handle.

In a small bowl, combine pistachio nuts and honey. Using a rolling pin, roll out half of dough between sheets of plastic wrap into an 8 x 10-inch rectangle. Spread dough with half of pistachio mixture to within 1/2 inch of edges. Beginning at 1 long edge, roll up dough jellyroll style. Repeat with remaining dough and pistachio mixture. Wrap in plastic wrap and chill 2 hours or until firm enough to slice.

Preheat oven to 375 degrees. If rolls have flattened on the bottom, reshape into a round shape. Using a serrated knife, cut dough into 1/4-inch slices. Place 1 inch apart on an ungreased baking sheet. Bake 9 to 11 minutes or until bottoms are lightly browned. Transfer cookies to a wire rack to cool. Store in an airtight container.

Yield: about 5 dozen cookies

PECAN-PRALINE BARS

CRUST
 3/4 cup butter or margarine, softened
 1/3 cup firmly packed brown sugar
 1 1/2 cups all-purpose flour

TOPPING
 1 1/2 cups firmly packed brown sugar
    3 eggs, beaten
    3 tablespoons all-purpose flour
 1/2 teaspoon baking powder
    3 tablespoons pecan liqueur
    1 teaspoon vanilla extract
 1 1/2 cups coarsely chopped pecans,
        toasted

Preheat oven to 350 degrees. For crust, cream butter and brown sugar in a medium bowl until fluffy. Add flour; stir until well blended. Press crust into bottom of a lightly greased 9 x 13-inch baking pan. Bake 12 minutes.

For topping, combine brown sugar and eggs in a medium bowl; beat until well blended. In a small bowl, combine flour and baking powder. Add dry ingredients, liqueur, and vanilla to brown sugar mixture; stir until well blended. Stir in pecans. Pour filling over warm crust. Bake 25 to 30 minutes or until center is set and top is golden brown. Place pan on a wire rack to cool. Cut into 1 x 2-inch bars. Store in an airtight container.

Yield: about 4 dozen bars

SPICED FRUIT RAVIOLI COOKIES

COOKIES

- 1/2 cup butter or margarine, softened
- 1/2 cup granulated sugar
- 1 egg
- 1 tablespoon orange juice
- 1 teaspoon grated orange zest
- 1 teaspoon vanilla extract
- 2 1/2 cups all-purpose flour
- 1/4 cup sifted confectioners sugar
- 2 tablespoons cornstarch

FILLING

- 1/3 cup coarsely chopped dried peaches
- 1/3 cup sugar
- 1/4 cup water
- 1 tablespoon peach brandy
- 1/4 teaspoon ground allspice

For cookies, cream butter and granulated sugar in a large bowl until fluffy. Add egg, orange juice, orange zest, and vanilla; beat until smooth. In a small bowl, combine flour, confectioners sugar, and cornstarch. Add dry ingredients to creamed mixture; stir until a soft dough forms. Divide dough into balls. Wrap in plastic wrap and chill hours or until firm enough to handle.

For filling, combine peaches, sugar, and water in a heavy small saucepan over high heat. Stirring frequently, bring to a boil. Reduce heat to low and cover. Stirring occasionally, simmer 10 to 12 minutes or until most of liquid is absorbed. Stir in peach brandy and allspice. Place peach mixture in a food processor. Pulse process until coarsely puréed; set aside.

Using a rolling pin, roll 1 ball of dough between sheets of plastic wrap into a inch circle. Remove top sheet of plastic wrap. Using a 2-inch round ravioli cutter, lightly mark circles on dough. Place teaspoonful of peach mixture in center of each circle. Roll out second piece of dough between sheets of plastic wrap.

A fruity filling of dried peaches, brandy, and allspice is layered between two sheets of orange-flavored pastry to make our tasty Spiced Fruit Ravioli Cookies.

Remove top sheet of plastic wrap and invert dough on top of peach-topped dough, matching edges. (There should be 2 layers of dough between 2 sheets of plastic wrap.) Transfer plastic-covered dough onto a baking sheet; chill 20 minutes. Preheat oven to 350 degrees. Remove top sheet of plastic wrap. Using ravioli cutter and keeping filling in center of cutter, cut out cookies. Use a spatula to carefully transfer cookies to a greased baking sheet. Bake 8 to 10 minutes or until edges are lightly browned. Transfer cookies to a wire rack to cool. Repeat with remaining dough and filling. Store in an airtight container.

Yield: about 3 dozen cookies

Light, delicate Amaretto Florentines are laced with liqueur and laden with sliced almonds.

AMARETTO FLORENTINES

- 3 tablespoons butter
- 1/3 cup sugar
- 2 tablespoons whipping cream
- 1 cup sliced almonds
- 1/4 cup all-purpose flour
- 2 tablespoons amaretto

Preheat oven to 350 degrees. In a heavy medium saucepan, combine butter, sugar, and whipping cream over medium-high heat. Stirring frequently, bring mixture to a boil. Remove from heat; cool to room temperature. Add almonds, flour, and amaretto; stir until well blended. Drop teaspoonfuls of dough 4 inches apart onto a baking sheet lined with parchment paper. Spread dough with back of spoon to form a thin layer. Bake 5 to 7 minutes or until edges are lightly browned. Leaving cookies on parchment paper, remove paper from

pan. Cool cookies 3 minutes; transfer to a wire rack to cool completely. Store in single layers between sheets of waxed paper in an airtight container.

Yield: about 3 1/2 dozen cookies

ORANGE CAPPUCCINO COOKIES

COOKIES

- 1 tablespoon instant coffee granules
- 1 tablespoon hot water
- 1/2 cup butter or margarine, softened
- 3/4 cup granulated sugar
- 1/4 cup firmly packed brown sugar
- 1 egg
- 1 teaspoon orange zest
- 1/2 teaspoon orange extract
- 1/2 teaspoon vanilla extract
- 2 cups all-purpose flour
- 1 teaspoon baking powder
- 1/2 teaspoon ground cinnamon
- 1/8 teaspoon salt

ICING

- 3 1/2 teaspoons instant coffee granules
- 2 1/2 tablespoons hot water
- 2 cups sifted confectioners sugar

For cookies, dissolve instant coffee in hot water in a small bowl; set aside. In a large bowl, cream butter and sugars until fluffy. Add egg, orange zest, extracts, and coffee mixture; beat until smooth. In a small bowl, combine flour, baking powder, cinnamon, and salt. Add dry ingredients to creamed mixture; stir until a soft dough forms. Cover dough and chill 2 hours or until firm enough to handle.

Preheat oven to 375 degrees. Shape dough into 1-inch balls. Place 2 inches apart on a lightly greased baking sheet. Slightly flatten balls to 1 3/4-inch diameter with greased bottom of a glass. Bake 7 to 9 minutes or until bottoms are lightly

browned. Transfer cookies to a wire rack with waxed paper underneath to cool.

For icing, dissolve instant coffee in hot water in a medium bowl. Add confectioner sugar; stir until smooth. Ice cookies. Allow icing to harden. Store in single layers between sheets of waxed paper in an airti[ght] container.

Yield: about 4 dozen cookies

ANISE SEED BISCOTTI

- 1/2 cup butter or margarine, softened
- 1 cup sugar
- 3 eggs
- 1 tablespoon lemon zest
- 1 teaspoon lemon extract
- 3 cups all-purpose flour
- 1 tablespoon anise seed
- 1 teaspoon baking powder
- 1/2 teaspoon baking soda
- 1/8 teaspoon salt

Preheat oven to 375 degrees. In a large bowl, cream butter and sugar until fluffy. Add eggs, lemon zest, and lemon extract; beat until smooth. In a medium bowl, combine flour, anise seed, baking powder baking soda, and salt. Add dry ingredient to creamed mixture; stir until a soft dough forms.

Divide dough in half. On a greased and floured baking sheet, shape each piece of dough into a 2 1/2 x 10-inch loaf, flouring hands as necessary. Allow 3 inches betwe[en] loaves on baking sheet. Bake 25 to 28 minutes or until loaves are lightly browned; cool 10 minutes on baking shee[t]. Cut loaves diagonally into 1/2-inch slices. Place slices flat on an ungreased baking sheet. Bake 5 to 7 minutes; turn slices ove[r] and bake 5 to 7 minutes longer or until lightly browned. Transfer cookies to a wir[e] rack to cool. Store in a cookie tin.

Yield: about 2 1/2 dozen cookies

Orange Cappuccino Cookies (from left) *are topped with coffee-flavored icing for an after-dinner sweet. Kissed with* a *splash of bourbon and rolled in ground pecans, Chocolate-Nut Truffle Cookies are an irresistible treat. Anise Seed* Biscotti *will fill your home with the citrusy aroma of lemon and licorice. These toasted cookies are even better when* dunked *in a cup of hot coffee, tea, or cocoa!*

CHOCOLATE-NUT TRUFFLE COOKIES

1   cup butter or margarine, softened
    and divided
3/4 cup whipping cream
2   tablespoons honey
1   package (6 ounces) semisweet
    chocolate chips
2   tablespoons bourbon
1   teaspoon vanilla extract
1/2 cup sifted confectioners sugar
3/4 cups all-purpose flour
1/4 teaspoon ground nutmeg
1/4 teaspoon salt

1 1/2 cups chopped pecans, toasted
       and coarsely ground

In a heavy medium saucepan, combine 1/4 cup butter, whipping cream, and honey over medium-low heat. Stirring frequently, heat mixture to a simmer. Remove from heat. Add chocolate chips; stir until smooth. Stir in bourbon and vanilla. In a large bowl, cream remaining 3/4 cup butter and confectioners sugar until fluffy. In a medium bowl, combine flour, nutmeg, and salt. Add

dry ingredients and chocolate mixture to creamed mixture; stir until a soft dough forms. Cover dough and chill 1 hour.

Preheat oven to 375 degrees. Shape dough into 1-inch balls and roll in pecans. Transfer to an ungreased baking sheet. Bake 6 to 8 minutes or until firm. Transfer cookies to a wire rack to cool. Store in an airtight container.

Yield: about 6 1/2 dozen cookies

PALMIERS

Sugar
1 package (17¼ ounces) frozen
    puff pastry, thawed according to
    package directions

Preheat oven to 400 degrees. Lightly sprinkle sugar on a sheet of plastic wrap. Using a rolling pin, roll 1 sheet of pastry dough into a 9½ x 12-inch rectangle about ⅛-inch thick on sugared plastic wrap. Cut dough in half lengthwise. Fold long edges of each dough strip to almost meet at center. Fold dough in half lengthwise. Cut dough into ½-inch crosswise slices. Dip 1 cut side of each slice in sugar. Place sugared side down on an ungreased baking sheet. Bake 7 minutes. Remove from oven and lightly sprinkle with sugar. Turn slices over and bake 7 minutes longer. Transfer cookies to a wire rack to cool. Repeat with remaining sheet of dough. Store in a cookie tin.

Yield: about 8 dozen cookies

BLACK FOREST BROWNIES

BROWNIES
¾ cup dried cherries (available at
    gourmet food stores)
3 tablespoons kirsch (cherry liqueur)
1 package (19.8 ounces) brownie
    mix
⅓ cup vegetable oil
2 eggs, beaten
2 tablespoons water

ICING
1 package (6 ounces) semisweet
    chocolate chips
2 tablespoons butter or margarine
2 tablespoons light corn syrup
2 tablespoons kirsch (cherry liqueur)

For brownies, combine cherries and kirsch in a small bowl; allow to stand 30 minutes.

Topped with a dark chocolate frosting and layered with dried cherries, our Black Forest Brownies (left) are a chocolate lover's delight. Purchased puff pastry dough is simply sprinkled with sugar to create light and tasty Palmiers.

Preheat oven to 350 degrees. In a large bowl, combine brownie mix, oil, eggs, water, and cherry mixture; stir until well blended. Line a 9 x 13-inch baking pan with aluminum foil, extending foil over ends of pan; grease foil. Spread batter into prepared pan. Bake 20 to 25 minutes or until brownies start to pull away from sides of pan. Place pan on a wire rack to cool. Use ends of foil to lift brownies from pan.

For icing, melt chocolate chips and butter in a heavy small saucepan over low heat, stirring frequently. Remove from hea[t.] Add corn syrup and kirsch; beat until smooth. Spread warm icing over brownie[s;] allow icing to harden. Cut into 1½ x 2-in[ch] bars. Store in an airtight container.

Yield: about 3½ dozen brownies

RASPBERRY-ALMOND BARS

CRUST

- 1/2 cup butter or margarine, softened
- 1/2 cup firmly packed brown sugar
- 1 teaspoon vanilla extract
- 1/2 cups all-purpose flour
- 1/3 cup seedless raspberry jam

FILLING

- 1/2 cup almond paste, coarsely crumbled
- 1/2 cup sugar
- 2 eggs
- 1 teaspoon vanilla extract
- 1 cup sliced almonds, coarsely chopped

Preheat oven to 350 degrees. For crust, cream butter, brown sugar, and vanilla in a medium bowl. Add flour to creamed mixture; stir until well blended. Press dough into a greased 9 x 13-inch baking pan. Spread jam over dough.

For filling, combine almond paste and sugar in a medium bowl until well blended. Add eggs and vanilla; beat until smooth. Spread filling over jam. Sprinkle almonds over filling, pressing lightly into filling. Bake 20 to 25 minutes or until filling is lightly browned around edges. Cool in pan on a wire rack. Cut into 1 x 2-inch bars. Store in an airtight container.

Yield: about 4 dozen bars

CHOCOLATE ADDICTIONS

- 4 ounces semisweet baking chocolate, coarsely chopped
- 4 ounces unsweetened baking chocolate, coarsely chopped
- 3 tablespoons unsalted butter or margarine
- 1/4 cup sugar
- 3 eggs
- 1 teaspoon vanilla extract
- 1/3 cup all-purpose flour

A wonderful way to end the evening's festivities, Raspberry-Almond Bars (left) feature a nutty filling nestled between a fruity crust and a sliced-almond topping. Chopped walnuts and chocolate chips are mixed into a chocolaty batter to make our Chocolate Addictions a luscious indulgence.

- 1/4 teaspoon baking powder
- 1 1/2 cups coarsely chopped walnuts
- 1 package (6 ounces) semisweet chocolate chips

Preheat oven to 350 degrees. Place baking chocolate and butter in top of double boiler over, but not touching, hot water. Stir until chocolate and butter are melted. Remove from heat and allow to cool. In a small bowl, beat sugar, eggs, and vanilla until smooth. Stir in chocolate mixture. In a small bowl, combine flour and baking powder. Add dry ingredients to creamed mixture; stir until a soft dough forms. Stir in walnuts and chocolate chips. Drop teaspoonfuls of dough 2 inches apart onto a baking sheet lined with parchment paper. Bake 7 to 8 minutes or until lightly browned on bottom. Leaving cookies on parchment paper, remove paper from pan. Cool cookies 5 minutes; transfer to a wire rack to cool completely. Store in an airtight container.

Yield: about 7 dozen cookies

AROUND THE WORLD

You don't have to travel halfway around the world to sample the authentic flavor of international sweets! This well-traveled collection includes traditional favorites that are steeped in the heritage of faraway lands such as Scotland, Greece, and Germany, and as nearby as the Canadian border. You'll delight in the simple taste of Scottish Shortbread and marvel over the creamy, full-bodied flavor of Nanaimo Bars. Our twelve delectable desserts from abroad are sure to please family, friends, and neighbors.

Chocolate Madeleines	Pfeffernüsse
Turkish Almond Cookies	Austrian Linzer Bars
Greek Kourabiedes	Scandinavian Cardamom Cookies
Moravian Spice Cookies	Nanaimo Bars
German Lebkuchen	French Sablés
Scottish Shortbread	French Almond Tuiles

(Previous page) *Moravian Spice Cookies* (from left) are thin, crispy sweets flavored with molasses and five different spices. Ground almonds, confectioners sugar, and egg whites are combined to create Turkish Almond Cookies. Before baking Greek Kourabiedes, whole cloves are placed in the centers to give these melt-in-your-mouth cookies their delightful taste. Chocolate Madeleines, a French favorite, are delicious sponge cake morsels laced with cherry liqueur.

CHOCOLATE MADELEINES

- $3/4$ cup granulated sugar
- 2 eggs
- 2 egg yolks
- 2 tablespoons kirsch (cherry liqueur)
- 1 teaspoon vanilla extract
- 1 cup all-purpose flour
- $1/4$ cup Dutch process cocoa
- $1/8$ teaspoon salt
- $1/2$ cup butter or margarine, melted and cooled
   Confectioners sugar

Preheat oven to 400 degrees. In a large bowl, beat granulated sugar, eggs, and egg yolks 5 minutes or until mixture is thick and light in color. Stir in kirsch and vanilla. In a small bowl, combine flour, cocoa, and salt. Sift dry ingredients over egg mixture; fold in dry ingredients. Fold melted butter into batter. Spoon 1 tablespoon of batter into each greased 2 x 3-inch mold of a madeleine pan. Bake 6 to 8 minutes or until madeleines spring back when lightly touched. Transfer cookies to a wire rack. Lightly sift confectioners sugar over warm cookies; cool. Store in an airtight container.

Yield: about $2^{1}/2$ dozen cookies

TURKISH ALMOND COOKIES

- 1 cup slivered almonds
- 2 cups sifted confectioners sugar
- 3 egg whites
   Whole almonds

Place slivered almonds in food processor; process until almost finely ground. Add confectioners sugar; process until well blended. In a heavy medium saucepan, combine sugar mixture and egg whites. Attach a candy thermometer to saucepan, making sure thermometer does not touch bottom of pan. Stirring frequently, cook over medium heat until mixture reaches 130 degrees. Pour into a medium bowl and cool to room temperature.

Preheat oven to 300 degrees. Spoon mixture into a pastry bag fitted with a medium round tip. Pipe 1-inch-diameter cookies 2 inches apart onto a baking sheet lined with parchment paper. Place a whole almond on top of each cookie. Bake 20 to 25 minutes or until tops are lightly browned. Cool cookies on pan 5 minutes; transfer to a wire rack to cool completely. Store in an airtight container.

Yield: about 4 dozen cookies

GREEK KOURABIEDES

- 2 cups butter, softened
- $3/4$ cup sifted confectioners sugar
- 1 egg yolk
- 1 teaspoon vanilla extract
- $4^{1}/2$ cups all-purpose flour
   Whole cloves
   Confectioners sugar

Preheat oven to 350 degrees. In a large bowl, cream butter and $3/4$ cup confectioners sugar until fluffy. Add egg yolk and vanilla; beat until smooth. Add flour; stir until a soft dough forms. Shape dough into 1-inch balls and place 1 inch apart on an ungreased baking sheet. Press

1 whole clove in top of each cookie. Bake 15 to 17 minutes or until lightly browned bottom. Transfer cookies to a wire rack. confectioners sugar over warm cookies; cool. Store in an airtight container.

Yield: about 8 dozen cookies

MORAVIAN SPICE COOKIES

It's best if dough is made in advance.

- $1/2$ cup butter or margarine, softened
- $1/3$ cup firmly packed brown sugar
- 1 cup molasses
- $3^{1}/2$ cups all-purpose flour
- $3/4$ teaspoon baking soda
- $3/4$ teaspoon ground ginger
- $3/4$ teaspoon ground cloves
- $3/4$ teaspoon ground cinnamon
- $1/4$ teaspoon ground nutmeg
- $1/4$ teaspoon ground allspice
- $1/4$ teaspoon salt

In a large bowl, cream butter and brown sugar until fluffy. Add molasses; beat until smooth. In a medium bowl, combine flour, baking soda, ginger, cloves, cinnamon, nutmeg, allspice, and salt. Gradually add ingredients to creamed mixture; stir until soft dough forms. Divide dough into four. Wrap in plastic wrap and chill 48 hours or up to 1 week.

Preheat oven to 350 degrees. On a heavily floured surface, use a floured rolling pin to roll out one fourth of dough to $1/16$-inch thickness. Use a $1^{7}/8$-inch-diameter fluted-edge cookie cutter to cut out cookies. Transfer to a greased baking sheet. Bake 4 to 6 minutes or until edges are lightly browned. Transfer cookies to a wire rack cool. Repeat with remaining dough. Store a cookie tin.

Yield: about 19 dozen cookies

Drizzled with delicate lemon icing, traditional German Lebkuchen cookies combine the tastes of honey, cocoa, and ces. We used a scalloped heart-shaped cookie cutter to give ours a pretty look.

ERMAN LEBKUCHEN

OKIES

1/2 cups butter, softened
3/4 cup honey
3/4 cup sugar
 1 egg
 2 tablespoons grated lemon zest
 1 teaspoon vanilla extract
 4 cups all-purpose flour
 2 tablespoons cocoa
 2 teaspoons ground cinnamon
 1 teaspoon ground allspice
 1 teaspoon ground cloves
 1 teaspoon ground ginger
1/4 teaspoon ground cardamom
1/4 teaspoon baking powder
1/4 teaspoon baking soda

ICING

1 1/4 cups sifted confectioners sugar
 1 tablespoon lemon juice
 1 tablespoon water

For cookies, cream butter, honey, and sugar in a large bowl. Add egg, lemon zest, and vanilla; beat until smooth. In a medium bowl, combine flour, cocoa, cinnamon, allspice, cloves, ginger, cardamom, baking powder, and baking soda. Add dry ingredients to creamed mixture; stir until a soft dough forms. Divide dough into fourths. Wrap in plastic wrap and chill overnight or until firm enough to handle.

Preheat oven to 350 degrees. On a lightly floured surface, use a floured rolling pin to roll out one fourth of dough to 1/4-inch thickness. Use a 3 1/2-inch heart-shaped cookie cutter to cut out cookies. Transfer to a lightly greased baking sheet. Bake 8 to 10 minutes or until edges are lightly browned. Transfer cookies to a wire rack with waxed paper underneath to cool. Repeat with remaining dough.

For icing, combine all ingredients in a small bowl; stir until smooth. Spoon icing into a pastry bag fitted with a very small round tip. Pipe desired decorations onto cookies. Allow icing to harden. Store in an airtight container.

Yield: about 3 dozen cookies

PFEFFERNÜSSE

    2 eggs
 2¼ cups firmly packed brown sugar
    1 tablespoon milk
  ½ teaspoon baking soda
    2 cups all-purpose flour
  ½ teaspoon ground cinnamon
  ¼ teaspoon ground nutmeg
  ¼ teaspoon ground white pepper
    1 cup finely chopped pecans

In a large bowl, beat eggs. Add brown sugar; beat until well blended. In a small bowl, combine milk and baking soda; stir into brown sugar mixture. In a small bowl combine flour, cinnamon, nutmeg, and white pepper. Add dry ingredients to sugar mixture; stir until a soft dough forms. Stir pecans. On a lightly floured surface, use a floured rolling pin to roll out dough to ¼-inch thickness. Use a doughnut hole cutter to cut out cookies. Transfer to a greased baking sheet. Cover lightly and allow cookies to sit at room temperature overnight.

Preheat oven to 350 degrees. Bake 3 minutes. Remove from oven and drop pan onto a heat-resistant, flat surface to flatten cookies. Return to oven and bake 5 minutes longer or until bottoms are lightly browned. Transfer cookies to a wire rack to cool. Store in an airtight container.

Yield: about 6½ dozen cookies

AUSTRIAN LINZER BARS

    1 cup butter or margarine, softened
  ¾ cup sugar
    2 egg yolks
    1 tablespoon grated lemon zest
    1 teaspoon vanilla extract
    2 cups all-purpose flour
    1 teaspoon ground cinnamon
  ½ teaspoon baking powder
  ½ teaspoon ground allspice
    1 cup sliced almonds, finely ground

Sweet, spicy Pfeffernüsse (in jar), or Peppernuts, are a crunchy German specialty made with brown sugar, pecans, and white pepper. Rich and buttery, Scottish Shortbread is an easy-to-make delicacy for cold winter afternoons. The decorative edges are simple to create with a fork.

SCOTTISH SHORTBREAD

    1 cup butter, softened
  ¼ cup plus 2 tablespoons sifted
         confectioners sugar
  ¼ cup firmly packed brown sugar
    2 cups all-purpose flour

Preheat oven to 325 degrees. In a large bowl, cream butter and sugars until fluffy. Gradually add flour and stir just until well blended (do not overmix). Shape dough into 2 balls. Press half of dough onto a sheet of parchment paper to a diameter of 7½ inches. Place paper with dough circle on a baking sheet; repeat with remaining dough. Using a fork, press edges of dough and prick tops several times. Bake 23 to 25 minutes or until edges are lightly browned. Transfer pan to a wire rack. Cool 10 minutes; transfer parchment paper with shortbread onto a hard cutting surface. Cut each warm shortbread round into 8 wedges; cool completely. Store in an airtight container.

Yield: 16 shortbread wedges

1   cup seedless raspberry jam
1   cup sliced almonds, coarsely
      chopped

Preheat oven to 375 degrees. In a large
[b]owl, cream butter and sugar until fluffy.
[Ad]d egg yolks, lemon zest, and vanilla; beat
[un]til smooth. In a small bowl, combine
[flo]ur, cinnamon, baking powder, and
[all]spice. Add dry ingredients to creamed
[m]ixture; stir until a soft dough forms. Stir
[in] ground almonds. Press dough into a
[gr]eased 9 x 13-inch baking pan. Spread
[ra]spberry jam over dough. Sprinkle
[co]arsely chopped almonds over jam.
[Ba]ke 28 to 30 minutes or until edges are
[br]owned. Cool in pan. Cut into 1 x 2-inch
[ba]rs. Store in an airtight container.

[Yi]eld: about 4 dozen bars

[S]CANDINAVIAN CARDAMOM [C]OOKIES

3/4   cup butter, softened
1/2   cup granulated sugar
1/2   teaspoon lemon extract
3/4   cups all-purpose flour
1/2   teaspoons ground cardamom,
        divided
1/4   teaspoon ground ginger
1/2   cup sliced almonds, coarsely
        chopped
1/4   cup sifted confectioners sugar
        Sliced almonds

Preheat oven to 375 degrees. In a large
[bo]wl, cream butter, granulated sugar, and
[le]mon extract until fluffy. In a small bowl,
[co]mbine flour, 1 teaspoon cardamom, and
[gi]nger. Add dry ingredients to creamed
[m]ixture; stir until mixture resembles fine
[m]eal. Stir in chopped almonds. Press
[m]ixture into 1-inch balls. In a medium
[bo]wl, combine confectioners sugar and
[re]maining 1 1/2 teaspoons cardamom. Roll
[ba]lls in confectioners sugar mixture and
[pl]ace 2 inches apart on a greased baking

Crowned with a bit of powdered sugar for a tempting surprise, crispy Cardamom Cookies (top) are spiced with ground cardamom, a popular ingredient with Scandinavian cooks. Austrian Linzer Bars have a nutty crust and a topping of raspberry jam and sliced almonds.

sheet. Flatten with bottom of a glass dipped in confectioners sugar mixture. Insert sides of sliced almonds into cookies. Bake 8 to 10 minutes or until bottoms are lightly browned. Transfer cookies to a wire rack to cool. Store in an airtight container.

Yield: about 3 1/2 dozen cookies

Named for a city in British Columbia, Canadian Nanaimo Bars (right) *consist of three sumptuous layers: a chocolaty coconut-walnut crust, a buttercream filling, and a dark chocolate topping. French Sablés are flavored with lemon zest and toasted ground almonds.*

NANAIMO BARS

FILLING

- 1/3 cup sugar
- 2 tablespoons water
- 2 egg yolks, beaten
- 1/2 teaspoon vanilla extract
- 1/2 teaspoon orange extract
- 1/2 cup butter, softened

CRUST

- 1/2 cup butter or margarine
- 1/2 cup semisweet chocolate chips
- 1 cup sweetened shredded coconut
- 1 cup graham cracker crumbs
- 1 cup finely chopped walnuts

TOPPING

- 1/2 cup semisweet chocolate chips
- 2 teaspoons vegetable shortening

For filling, combine sugar and water in a heavy small saucepan. Bring to a boil over medium-high heat. Remove from heat. Stir a small amount of hot sugar mixture into egg yolks. Stirring constantly, return egg yolk mixture to saucepan and bring to a boil over medium heat; reduce heat to low. Stirring constantly, cook 2 minutes. Remove from heat. Stir in extracts. Pour into a small bowl; chill. In a medium bowl, cream butter until fluffy. Add chilled egg mixture; beat until smooth. Set aside.

For crust, melt butter in a heavy medium saucepan over low heat. Add chocolate chips, stirring until melted. Remove from heat. Stir in coconut, cracker crumbs, and alnuts. Press mixture into a greased 9-inch square baking pan. Chill in pan 5 minutes to allow chocolate to harden. Spread filling over crust; cover and chill 20 minutes.

For topping, melt chocolate chips and shortening in a heavy small saucepan over low heat. Remove from heat. Drizzle chocolate over chilled filling. Chill until chocolate has hardened. Cut into 1¹/₂-inch squares. Store in an airtight container in refrigerator.

Yield: about 3 dozen bars

FRENCH SABLÉS

³/₄ cup butter or margarine, softened
¹/₂ cup granulated sugar
¹/₄ cup sifted confectioners sugar
 1 egg
 1 egg yolk
 2 teaspoons grated lemon zest
2¹/₂ cups all-purpose flour
²/₃ cup slivered almonds, toasted and
      finely ground

In a large bowl, cream butter and sugars until fluffy. Add egg, egg yolk, and lemon zest; beat until smooth. In a medium bowl, combine flour and ground almonds. Add dry ingredients to creamed mixture; stir until a soft dough forms. Divide dough in half. Wrap in plastic wrap and chill 1 hour or until firm enough to handle.

Preheat oven to 350 degrees. On a lightly floured surface, use a floured rolling pin to roll out half of dough to ¹/₄-inch thickness. Use a 2¹/₂-inch-diameter fluted-edge cookie cutter to cut out cookies. Transfer to a greased baking sheet. Bake 10 to 12 minutes or until bottoms are lightly browned. Transfer cookies to a wire rack to cool. Repeat with remaining dough. Store in an airtight container.

Yield: about 3 dozen cookies

French Almond Tuiles combine the licorice flavor of anise seed and the light, citrusy taste of orange and lemon zests. Baked until golden brown, the cookies are then draped over a rolling pin to form their curved shape as they cool.

FRENCH ALMOND TUILES

¹/₂ cup butter or margarine, softened
 1 cup sugar
 1 tablespoon grated orange zest
 1 tablespoon grated lemon zest
¹/₂ teaspoon vanilla extract
 4 egg whites
¹/₂ cup all-purpose flour
 2 teaspoons anise seed
1¹/₂ cups sliced almonds, toasted

Preheat oven to 400 degrees. In a large bowl, cream butter, sugar, orange zest, lemon zest, and vanilla until fluffy. While beating mixture, add egg whites; beat until well blended. Sift flour over egg white mixture; fold into mixture. Fold in anise seed. Drop heaping teaspoonfuls of batter 4 inches apart onto a baking sheet lined with parchment paper. Sprinkle about 1 teaspoon sliced almonds over each cookie. Bake 5 to 6 minutes or until edges are golden brown. Shape each cookie by immediately placing cookie over a rolling pin to cool slightly. Transfer cookies to a wire rack to cool completely. Store in an airtight container.

Yield: about 4 dozen cookies

GOOD FOR YOU!

With today's emphasis on healthy eating habits, it's no wonder that many of us are turning to lower-fat treats to satisfy our sweet tooth. Making snacks that are good for you has never been easier than with this collection of cookie recipes. You'll find some old favorites that won't add to your waistline, and you'll learn how to make your cookies extra moist with nutritious ingredients like nonfat yogurt and applesauce. Each recipe includes the calorie count you can expect per serving, plus a listing of protein, fat, and carbohydrate grams.

(Previous page) *For the old-fashioned taste of gingerbread without all the calories, try Chewy Spice Cookies (from left) topped with a zesty lemon icing. Wonderfully delicious, Chocolate-Oat Bars are made with only a drizzling of oil. Raisin-Nut Chewies are healthy treats that you can make in a jiffy with only four ingredients!*

CHOCOLATE-OAT BARS

- 1/4 cup vegetable oil
- 3/4 cup firmly packed brown sugar
- 1/3 cup granulated sugar
- 2 egg whites
- 2 teaspoons vanilla extract
- 1 1/2 cups all-purpose flour
- 1 cup quick-cooking oats
- 1/2 teaspoon baking soda
- 1/8 teaspoon salt
  Vegetable cooking spray
- 1/2 cup semisweet chocolate mini chips

Preheat oven to 375 degrees. In a large bowl, beat oil and sugars until well blended. Add egg whites and vanilla; beat until smooth. In a small bowl, combine flour, oats, baking soda, and salt. Add dry ingredients to sugar mixture; stir until well blended. Press dough into a 9 x 13-inch baking pan lightly sprayed with cooking spray. Sprinkle chocolate chips over top; press into dough. Bake 10 to 12 minutes or until lightly browned. Cool in pan. Cut into 1 x 2-inch bars. Store in an airtight container.

Yield: about 4 dozen bars

1 serving (1 bar): 59 calories, 2 grams fat, 0.6 gram protein, 7.5 grams carbohydrate

RAISIN-NUT CHEWIES

- 2 egg whites
- 1/2 cup sugar
- 2 1/2 cups raisin bran cereal
- 1/3 cup chopped pecans, toasted and coarsely ground

Preheat oven to 200 degrees. In a medium bowl, beat egg whites until soft peaks form. Gradually add sugar, beating until mixture is very stiff. Fold in cereal and pecans. Drop teaspoonfuls of mixture 1 inch apart onto a baking sheet lined with parchment paper. Bake 1 hour or until bottoms are lightly browned. Transfer cookies to a wire rack to cool. Store in an airtight container.

Yield: about 3 1/2 dozen cookies

1 serving (1 cookie): 26 calories, 0.6 gram fat, 0.5 gram protein, 5.2 grams carbohydrate

CHEWY SPICE COOKIES

COOKIES

- 1 cup sugar
- 1 cup molasses
- 1/4 cup applesauce
- 1/4 cup skim milk
- 2 tablespoons vegetable oil
- 1 teaspoon rum flavoring
- 3 1/2 cups all-purpose flour
- 1 1/2 teaspoons ground ginger
- 1 teaspoon baking soda
- 1/2 teaspoon ground cloves
- 1/2 teaspoon ground nutmeg
- 1/4 teaspoon ground allspice
- 1/8 teaspoon salt
  Vegetable cooking spray

ICING

- 4 cups sifted confectioners sugar
- 4 tablespoons plus 1 teaspoon skim milk
- 2 tablespoons lemon juice
- 2 tablespoons grated lemon zest

Preheat oven to 375 degrees. For cookies, beat sugar, molasses, applesauce, milk, oil, and rum flavoring in a large bowl until well blended. In a medium bowl, combine flour, ginger, baking soda, cloves, nutmeg, allspice, and salt. Add dry ingredients, one third at a time, to sugar mixture; stir until a soft dough forms. Spray hands with cooking spray. Shape teaspoonfuls of dough into balls and flatten slightly with fingers. Place 2 inches apart on a baking sheet lightly sprayed with cooking spray. Bake 6 to 8 minutes or until bottoms are lightly browned. Transfer cookies to a wire rack with waxed paper underneath to cool.

For icing, combine all ingredients in a medium bowl; stir until smooth. Ice cookies. Allow icing to harden. Store in an airtight container.

Yield: about 6 dozen cookies

1 serving (1 cookie): 70 calories, 0.5 gram fat, 0.7 gram protein, 16 grams carbohydrate

GUMDROP COOKIES

- 3 tablespoons vegetable oil
- 1/2 cup sugar
- 1/4 cup egg substitute (equivalent to 1 egg)
- 1 tablespoon grated orange zest
- 1 teaspoon vanilla extract
- 1 1/3 cups all-purpose flour
- 1/2 teaspoon baking powder
- 1/4 teaspoon salt
  Vegetable cooking spray
- 4 ounces small spiced gumdrops

In a large bowl, beat oil and sugar until well blended. Add egg substitute, orange zest, and vanilla; beat until smooth. In a small bowl, combine flour, baking powder and salt. Add dry ingredients to sugar mixture; stir until a soft dough forms. Cover and chill 1 hour.

Colorful candies add a bright touch to Gumdrop Cookies (in jar), sweet treats that get their zest from grated orange [pe]el. A healthy alternative, Banana-Raisin Bars combine the wholesome goodness of bananas, yogurt, oats, and raisins.

[P]reheat oven to 350 degrees. Lightly [spr]ay hands and baking sheet with cooking [spr]ay. Shape dough into 1-inch balls and [pla]ce 1 inch apart on prepared pan. Press a [gum]drop in center of each cookie. Bake [8 t]o 9 minutes or until bottoms are lightly [br]owned. Transfer cookies to a wire rack to [co]ol. Store in an airtight container.

[*Yie*]*ld:* about 3 dozen cookies

[*1 s*]*erving (1 cookie):* 52 calories,
[2.?] grams fat, 0.7 gram protein, 6.9 grams
[car]bohydrate

BANANA-RAISIN BARS

1/4	cup vegetable oil
1 1/4	cups mashed ripe bananas, (about 2 large bananas)
1/4	cup firmly packed brown sugar
1/3	cup plain nonfat yogurt
1	teaspoon vanilla extract
2	cups old-fashioned oats
1/4	cup all-purpose flour
1/2	teaspoon baking soda
1/8	teaspoon salt
2/3	cup golden raisins
	Vegetable cooking spray

Preheat oven to 325 degrees. In a large bowl, beat oil, bananas, and brown sugar until well blended. Add yogurt and vanilla; stir until smooth. In a small bowl, combine oats, flour, baking soda, and salt. Add dry ingredients to banana mixture; stir until well blended. Stir in raisins. Line a 9 x 13-inch baking pan with aluminum foil, extending foil over ends of pan; lightly spray foil with cooking spray. Spread batter into prepared pan. Bake 27 to 29 minutes or until lightly browned. Cool in pan. Lift from pan using ends of foil. Cut into 1 x 2-inch bars. Store in an airtight container.

Yield: about 4 dozen bars

1 serving (1 bar): 42 calories, 1.5 grams fat, 0.9 gram protein, 7.4 grams carbohydrate

Great for serving up romance on Valentine's Day or any time you want to share a little love, Sweet Hearts are cherry-flavored meringue confections piped in heart shapes. The cookies also make a fitting treat for a special friend who's dieting.

SWEET HEARTS

  4 egg whites
  1/2 teaspoon cream of tartar
  1 teaspoon cherry flavoring
  1 1/2 cups sifted confectioners sugar
    Pink paste food coloring

Use heart pattern, page 118, and a piece of white paper to trace as many hearts as size of paper will allow, leaving 1/2 inch between each heart.

In a large bowl, beat egg whites and cream of tartar until soft peaks form. Add cherry flavoring. Gradually add confectioners sugar, beating until mixture is very stiff. Tint pink. Spoon meringue into a large pastry bag fitted with a large open star tip. Place heart patterns under greased waxed paper and pipe meringue onto waxed paper, carefully moving patterns as necessary. Allow cookies to sit at room temperature 30 minutes. Carefully place waxed paper with hearts on a greased baking sheet.

Preheat oven to 200 degrees. Bake 2 hours. Leaving cookies on waxed paper, remove waxed paper from pan while cookies are warm; cool. Carefully peel away waxed paper. Store immediately in an airtight container.

Yield: about 5 1/2 dozen cookies

1 serving (1 cookie): 10 calories, 0 gram fat, 0.2 gram protein, 2.3 grams carbohydrate

CRANBERRY-ORANGE SQUARES

  1 cup fresh cranberries
  1 1/4 cups granulated sugar, divided
  1 cup all-purpose flour
  1/4 cup cornstarch
  1/2 teaspoon baking soda
  1/2 teaspoon salt
  1/2 cup nonfat buttermilk
  4 1/2 tablespoons orange juice, divided
  2 egg whites
  1 teaspoon grated orange zest
    Vegetable cooking spray
  1 cup sifted confectioners sugar

Preheat oven to 350 degrees. Combine cranberries and 1/4 cup granulated sugar in food processor. Process until cranberries are coarsely chopped. In a small bowl, combine remaining 1 cup granulated sugar, flour, cornstarch, baking soda, and salt. Add buttermilk, 2 tablespoons orange juice, egg whites, and orange zest to dry ingredients; stir until well blended. Stir in cranberry mixture. Line a 9 x 13-inch baking pan with waxed paper; lightly spray paper with cooking spray. Spread mixture into prepared pan. Bake 20 to 25 minutes or until lightly browned. Cool in pan on a wire rack. Combine confectioners sugar and remaining 2 1/2 tablespoons orange juice in a small bowl; stir until smooth. Drizzle icing over top. Allow icing to harden. Cut into 1 1/2-inch squares. Store in an airtight container.

Yield: about 4 dozen squares

1 serving (1 square): 46 calories, 0.2 gram fat, 0.4 gram protein, 9.8 grams carbohydrate

LEMON-CARDAMOM DROPS

COOKIES

- 4 ounces (1/2 of an 8-ounce package) nonfat cream cheese, softened
- 2 tablespoons butter, softened
- 1/4 cups sugar, divided
- 2 egg whites
- 1 tablespoon grated lemon zest
- 1 teaspoon vanilla extract
- 1/2 teaspoon lemon extract
- 1/4 cups all-purpose flour
- 3/4 teaspoon baking powder
- 1/2 teaspoon ground cardamom
- Vegetable cooking spray

ICING

- 3/4 cup sifted confectioners sugar
- 3 teaspoons skim milk
- 1/4 teaspoon vanilla extract

For cookies, beat cream cheese, butter, and 1 cup sugar in a large bowl until fluffy. Add egg whites, lemon zest, and extracts; beat until smooth. In a medium bowl, combine flour, baking powder, and cardamom. Add dry ingredients to creamed mixture; stir until a soft dough forms.

Preheat oven to 350 degrees. Place remaining 1/4 cup sugar in a small bowl. Drop teaspoonfuls of dough into sugar; roll dough into balls. Place balls 2 inches apart on a baking sheet lightly sprayed with cooking spray; flatten balls with bottom of a glass dipped in sugar. Bake 5 to 7 minutes or until bottoms are lightly browned. Transfer cookies to a wire rack with waxed paper underneath to cool.

For icing, combine all ingredients in a small bowl; stir until smooth. Drizzle icing over cookies. Allow icing to harden. Store in airtight container.

Yield: about 6 dozen cookies

serving (1 cookie): 37 calories, 0.4 gram , 0.7 gram protein, 7.6 grams rbohydrate

Drizzled with a fruity icing, Cranberry-Orange Squares (top) are bursting with the sweet, tangy taste of fresh cranberries and oranges. With less than half a gram of fat per cookie, delectable Lemon-Cardamom Drops are made with nonfat cream cheese.

well blended. Line a 9-inch square baking pan with aluminum foil, extending foil over opposite sides of pan; spray foil with cooking spray. Pour batter into prepared pan. Bake 34 to 36 minutes or until brownies pull away from sides of pan. Cool in pan. Use ends of foil to lift brownies from pan.

For icing, combine all ingredients in a small bowl. Spread icing over brownies. Cleaning knife frequently, cut into 1 1/2-inch squares. Store in an airtight container in a single layer.

Yield: about 2 1/2 dozen brownies

1 serving (1 brownie): 92 calories, 2 grams fat, 1.0 gram protein, 18 grams carbohydrate

Unbelievably delicious, Moist and Chewy Brownies are made with evaporated skimmed milk and egg substitute. Orange marmalade gives the brownies added moistness and the creamy icing its refreshing flavor.

MOIST AND CHEWY BROWNIES

BROWNIES
- 1/4 cup vegetable oil
- 1 cup granulated sugar
- 1/2 cup firmly packed brown sugar
- 1/2 cup egg substitute (equivalent to 2 eggs)
- 1/4 cup evaporated skimmed milk
- 2 tablespoons light corn syrup
- 2 tablespoons orange marmalade
- 1 teaspoon vanilla extract
- 1 1/4 cups all-purpose flour
- 1/4 cup cocoa
- 1/4 teaspoon salt
  Vegetable cooking spray

ICING
- 1/2 cup sifted confectioners sugar
- 2 tablespoons orange marmalade
- 1 tablespoon cocoa
- 1 teaspoon skim milk
- 1/2 teaspoon vanilla extract

Preheat oven to 350 degrees. For brownies, beat oil and sugars in a large bowl until well blended. Add egg substitute, evaporated milk, corn syrup, marmalade, and vanilla; beat until smooth. In a small bowl, combine flour, cocoa, and salt. Add dry ingredients to sugar mixture; stir until

FRUITY OATMEAL COOKIES

- 1/2 cup pitted prunes
- 1 medium Granny Smith apple, peeled, cored, and diced
- 1/4 cup hot water
- 1 1/2 cups sugar
- 1/2 cup egg substitute (equivalent to 2 eggs)
- 1/4 cup vegetable oil
- 1 teaspoon vanilla extract
- 2 cups all-purpose flour
- 1 teaspoon ground cinnamon
- 1 teaspoon baking soda
- 1/2 teaspoon baking powder
- 1/2 teaspoon salt
- 3 cups old-fashioned oats, toasted
- 1/3 cup chopped pecans, toasted
  Vegetable cooking spray

Preheat oven to 375 degrees. Combine prunes, apple, and hot water in food processor; process until smooth. In a large bowl, beat sugar, egg substitute, oil, and vanilla until well blended. Add prune mixture. In a small bowl, combine flour, cinnamon, baking soda, baking powder, and salt. Add dry ingredients to sugar

ture; stir until well blended. Stir in oats
pecans. Drop heaping teaspoonfuls of
gh 2 inches apart onto a baking sheet
tly sprayed with cooking spray. Bake 7
minutes or until edges are lightly
wned. Transfer cookies to a wire rack to
l. Store in an airtight container.

d: about 6 dozen cookies

rving (1 cookie): 55 calories,
grams fat, 1.1 grams protein, 9.7 grams
bohydrate

ISIN-MOLASSES COOKIES

OKIES

4 cup vegetable oil
2 cup molasses
2 cup firmly packed brown sugar
3 cup nonfat sour cream
3 egg whites
1 teaspoon vanilla extract
2 cups all-purpose flour
1 teaspoon baking soda
1 teaspoon ground cinnamon
4 teaspoon salt
4 cups raisins
Vegetable cooking spray

NG

2 cups sifted confectioners sugar
3 tablespoons plus 1 teaspoon skim
milk
1 tablespoon grated orange zest
2 teaspoon orange extract

Preheat oven to 375 degrees. For
kies, beat oil, molasses, and brown
ar in a large bowl until well blended.
sour cream, egg whites, and vanilla;
t until smooth. In a small bowl, combine
r, baking soda, cinnamon, and salt. Add
ingredients to molasses mixture; stir
l a soft dough forms. Stir in raisins.
p teaspoonfuls of dough 2 inches apart
o a baking sheet lightly sprayed with
king spray. Bake 5 to 7 minutes or until
toms are lightly browned. Transfer

Fruity Oatmeal Cookies (in jar) *are naturally good snacks — they're chock-full of old-fashioned oats, pitted prunes, fresh apple, and toasted pecans. Dimpled with sweet, juicy raisins and topped with a lightly flavored orange icing,* Raisin-Molasses Cookies *make a great dessert to serve with coffee.*

cookies to a wire rack with waxed paper underneath to cool.

For icing, combine confectioners sugar, 3 tablespoons milk, orange zest, and orange extract in a small bowl; stir until smooth, adding additional milk as necessary, 1/2 teaspoon at a time, to thin. Spoon icing over cookies. Allow icing to harden. Store in an airtight container.

Yield: about 5 dozen cookies

1 serving (1 cookie): 68 calories, 1.4 grams fat, 0.8 gram protein, 13.5 grams carbohydrate

COOKIES ON THE GO

This heartwarming sampling of goodies includes lots of recipes for sharing with friends who are always on the go. A surprise care package of delicious home-baked cookies is a nice pick-me-up for college students, summer campers, or long-distance friends. You'll also find special sweets shaped like postcards! Decorated with the names of various places to visit, they're retirement-party musts. Or convey a fond farewell to globe-trotting pals with cute palm tree-shaped cookies. Whether you enjoy strolling on the beach, playing cards, traveling, or hiking, there's a scrumptious treat to accompany all of life's little adventures.

Pecan Crispies	Seashell Sandies
Peanut Butter Postcards	Cinnamon Sailboats
Chocolate-Nut Chewies	Two-Tone Cookies
Bon Voyage Cookies	Fig Bars
Trail Cookies	Bridge Partners

(Previous page) *Sealed with a kiss of honey, Peanut Butter Postcards (from left)* are topped with yummy icing and colorful "addresses." *Refrigerated and then sliced and baked, Pecan Crispies get their texture from crisp rice cereal. Bits of toasted pecans add a pleasantly nutty flavor to Chocolate-Nut Chewies.*

PECAN CRISPIES

- 1 cup butter or margarine, softened
- 1 cup firmly packed brown sugar
- 1 cup granulated sugar
- 2 eggs
- 1 teaspoon vanilla-butter-nut flavoring
- 1½ cups all-purpose flour
- ½ teaspoon baking soda
- ½ teaspoon baking powder
- 2 cups quick-cooking oats
- 1½ cups crispy rice cereal
- 1 cup finely chopped toasted pecans

In a large bowl, cream butter and sugars until fluffy. Add eggs and vanilla-butter-nut flavoring; beat until smooth. In a small bowl, combine flour, baking soda, and baking powder. Add dry ingredients to creamed mixture. Stir in oats, cereal, and pecans. Shape dough into four 8-inch-long rolls. Wrap in plastic wrap and chill 2 hours.

Preheat oven to 325 degrees. Cut dough into ¼-inch slices. Place 2 inches apart on a greased baking sheet. Bake 8 to 10 minutes or until bottoms are lightly browned. Transfer cookies to a wire rack to cool. Store in a cookie tin.

Yield: about 8 dozen cookies

PEANUT BUTTER POSTCARDS

COOKIES

- ¾ cup butter or margarine, softened
- 1 cup smooth peanut butter
- 1 cup firmly packed brown sugar
- ¾ cup granulated sugar
- 2 eggs
- 2 tablespoons honey
- 1½ cups whole-wheat flour
- 1 cup all-purpose flour
- ½ teaspoon salt

ICING

- 4½ cups sifted confectioners sugar
- ¼ cup plus 2 to 2½ tablespoons milk, divided
- 3 tablespoons butter or margarine, softened
- 2 tablespoons honey
- 1 teaspoon clear vanilla (used in cake decorating)
  Black and red paste food coloring

Preheat oven to 350 degrees. For cookies, cream butter, peanut butter, and sugars in a large bowl; beat until fluffy. Add eggs and honey; beat until smooth. In a medium bowl, combine flours and salt. Add dry ingredients to creamed mixture; stir until a soft dough forms. Divide dough in half. Line a 10½ x 15½-inch jellyroll pan with aluminum foil; grease foil. Press half of dough into bottom of prepared pan. Bake 12 to 14 minutes or until lightly browned. Cool in pan 5 minutes. Lift from pan using ends of foil. Cut into nine 5 x 3¼-inch cookies while warm. Transfer cookies to a wire rack with waxed paper underneath to cool. Repeat with remaining dough.

For icing, combine confectioners sugar, ¼ cup plus 1 tablespoon milk, butter, honey, and vanilla in a medium bowl; beat until smooth. Place 3 tablespoons icing in a small bowl. Tint black. Spoon black icing into a pastry bag fitted with a small round tip. Add 1 tablespoon milk to white icing; add additional milk, ½ teaspoon at a time,

for desired consistency. Place 3 tablespoo white icing into a small bowl. Tint red. Spoon red icing into a pastry bag fitted wi a small round tip. Spread white icing over cookies. Allow icing to harden. Use red icing to make lines for postmark. For hearts, squeeze 2 dots of red icing side by side and use tip to pull icing down and together to form a heart. Pipe "addresses" with black icing. Allow icings to harden. Store in single layers between waxed pape in an airtight container.

Yield: 18 cookies

CHOCOLATE-NUT CHEWIES

- 1½ cups butter or margarine, softened
- 2 cups granulated sugar
- ½ cup firmly packed brown sugar
- 2 eggs
- 1½ teaspoons vanilla extract
- 2¼ cups all-purpose flour
- ¾ cup cocoa
- 2 teaspoons baking soda
- 1½ cups finely chopped toasted pecans
  Granulated sugar

In a large bowl, cream butter and sugar until fluffy. Add eggs and vanilla; beat unti smooth. In a medium bowl, combine flou cocoa, and baking soda. Add dry ingredients to creamed mixture; stir until soft dough forms. Stir in pecans. Divide dough into fourths. Wrap in plastic wrap and chill 2 hours.

Preheat oven to 375 degrees. Using one fourth dough at a time, shape into 1-inch balls and roll in granulated sugar. Place balls 3 inches apart on a lightly greased baking sheet. Bake 5 to 7 minutes or until edges are firm. Cool cookies on pan 3 minutes; transfer to a wire rack to cool completely. Store in an airtight container.

Yield: about 10 dozen cookies

Even seasoned travelers will get a kick out of these cute cookies! Decorated with green icing leaves and brown jelly bean "coconuts," palm tree-shaped Bon Voyage Cookies have a tropical look that's perfect for a going-away party.

BON VOYAGE COOKIES

COOKIES
- 1 cup butter or margarine, softened
- 1 cup granulated sugar
- 1/2 cup firmly packed brown sugar
- 2 eggs
- 1 teaspoon vanilla extract
- 1 teaspoon coconut extract
- 2 1/4 cups all-purpose flour
- 1 cup whole-wheat flour
- 2 teaspoons baking soda
- 1/2 teaspoon salt

ICING
- 2 cups sifted confectioners sugar
- 1/4 cup vegetable shortening
- 1 1/2 tablespoons milk
- 1 teaspoon vanilla extract
  Green liquid food coloring
  Brown jelly beans to decorate

For cookies, cream butter and sugars in a large bowl until fluffy. Add eggs and extracts; beat until smooth. In a medium bowl, combine flours, baking soda, and salt. Add dry ingredients to creamed mixture; stir until a soft dough forms. Divide dough into fourths. Wrap in plastic wrap and chill 1 hour.

Preheat oven to 350 degrees. On a lightly floured surface, use a floured rolling pin to roll out one fourth of dough to 1/8-inch thickness. Use a 3 1/4 x 3 3/4-inch palm tree-shaped cookie cutter to cut out cookies. Place 1 inch apart on a greased baking sheet. Bake 6 to 8 minutes or until bottoms are lightly browned. Transfer cookies to a wire rack to cool. Repeat with remaining dough.

For icing, combine confectioners sugar, shortening, milk, and vanilla in a small bowl; stir until smooth. Tint green. Spoon icing into a pastry bag fitted with a leaf tip (#67). Pipe icing onto cookies for leaves. Decorate with jelly beans. Allow icing to harden. Store in single layers between sheets of waxed paper in an airtight container.

Yield: about 6 dozen cookies

Packed with pecans, oats, and wheat germ, Trail Cookies are sure to give you that much-needed energy boost while out on the hiking path. Raisins and coconut make these tasty morsels naturally sweet and chewy.

TRAIL COOKIES

- 1/2 cup butter or margarine, softened
- 1/2 cup firmly packed brown sugar
- 1/2 cup granulated sugar
- 1 egg
- 1 teaspoon vanilla extract
- 3/4 cup all-purpose flour
- 3/4 cup wheat germ
- 1 teaspoon baking powder
- 1 cup raisins
- 1/2 cup chopped pecans
- 1/3 cup sweetened shredded coconut
- 1/3 cup old-fashioned oats

Preheat oven to 350 degrees. In a large bowl, cream butter and sugars until fluffy.

Add egg and vanilla; beat until smooth. In a small bowl, combine flour, wheat germ, and baking powder. Add dry ingredients to creamed mixture; stir until a soft dough forms. Stir in raisins, pecans, coconut, and oats. Drop heaping tablespoonfuls of dough 2 inches apart onto a greased baking sheet. Bake 11 to 13 minutes or until edges are lightly browned. Cool cookies on pan 5 minutes; transfer to a wire rack to cool completely. Store in an airtight container.

Yield: about 2 1/2 dozen cookies

SEASHELL SANDIES

- 3/4 cup butter or margarine, softened
- 3/4 cup sifted confectioners sugar
- 1/4 cup firmly packed brown sugar
- 1 egg
- 1 1/2 teaspoons vanilla extract
- 2 1/4 cups all-purpose flour
- 1/2 cup chopped pecans, toasted and finely ground
- 1/4 teaspoon salt

In a large bowl, cream butter and sugar until fluffy. Add egg and vanilla; beat until smooth. In a medium bowl, combine flour, pecans, and salt. Add dry ingredients to creamed mixture; stir until a soft dough forms. Divide dough in half. Wrap in plastic wrap and chill 1 hour.

Preheat oven to 350 degrees. On a lightly floured surface, use a floured rolling pin to roll out half of dough to 1/4-inch thickness. Use a 3 1/2 x 2 3/4-inch seashell-shaped cookie cutter to cut out cookies. Transfer to an ungreased baking sheet. Bake 7 to 9 minutes or until bottoms are lightly browned. Transfer cookies to a wire rack to cool. Repeat with remaining dough. Store in an airtight container.

Yield: about 2 1/2 dozen cookies

CINNAMON SAILBOATS

COOKIES

- 1 cup butter or margarine, softened
- 1 1/2 cups granulated sugar
- 1/2 cup firmly packed brown sugar
- 4 eggs
- 1 1/2 tablespoons milk
- 1 1/2 teaspoons vanilla extract
- 4 1/4 cups all-purpose flour
- 1 1/2 teaspoons ground cinnamon
- 3/4 teaspoon baking powder
- 1/2 teaspoon baking soda
- 1/2 teaspoon salt

4 cups sifted confectioners sugar

⅓ cup milk

1 teaspoon clear vanilla extract
   (used in cake decorating)

2 tubes (4.25 ounces each)
   purchased blue decorating icing

For cookies, cream butter and sugars in
large bowl until fluffy. Add eggs, milk, and
vanilla; beat until smooth. In a medium
bowl, combine flour, cinnamon, baking
powder, baking soda, and salt. Add dry
ingredients to creamed mixture; stir until a
soft dough forms. Divide dough into fourths.
Wrap in plastic wrap and chill 3 hours or
until firm enough to handle.

Preheat oven to 400 degrees. On a lightly
floured surface, use a floured rolling pin to
roll out one fourth of dough to slightly
greater than ⅛-inch thickness. Use a
x 3½-inch sailboat-shaped cookie cutter
to cut out cookies. Place 2 inches apart on
lightly greased baking sheet. Bake 5 to
minutes or until edges are lightly
browned. Transfer cookies to a wire rack
with waxed paper underneath to cool.
Repeat with remaining dough.

For icing, combine confectioners sugar,
milk, and vanilla in a medium bowl; stir
until smooth. Ice sails on cookies; allow
icing to harden. Transfer decorating icing
to a pastry bag fitted with a small basket
weave tip. With flat side of tip up, pipe
icing stripes onto sails. Allow icing to
harden. Store in single layers between
sheets of waxed paper in an airtight
container.

Yield: about 6 dozen cookies

Decorated with racing stripes of blue icing, Cinnamon Sailboats (top) *are made with two favorite ingredients — cinnamon and brown sugar. Ground pecans give Seashell Sandies their rich taste. Shaped like shoreline treasures, the buttery shortbread cookies are ideal for a day at the beach.*

Two-Tone Cookies (left) *offer a delicious flavor combination. The dark side is loaded with semisweet chocolate chips, and the light side is bursting with pecans. For a sweet snack, pack our soft, chewy Fig Bars in your loved one's lunch box.*

TWO-TONE COOKIES

1 cup butter or margarine, softened
³/₄ cup granulated sugar
³/₄ cup firmly packed brown sugar
2 eggs
2 teaspoons vanilla extract
2 cups all-purpose flour
¹/₄ teaspoon baking soda
3 ounces semisweet baking chocolate, melted and cooled
1 cup semisweet chocolate mini chips
1 cup chopped pecans, toasted

Preheat oven to 375 degrees. In a large bowl, cream butter and sugars until fluffy. Add eggs and vanilla; beat until smooth. In a small bowl, combine flour and baking soda. Add dry ingredients to creamed mixture; stir until a soft dough forms. Divide dough in half, adding melted chocolate and chocolate chips to half of dough. Add pecans to remaining half of dough. Drop 1 tablespoonful of light dough onto a lightly greased baking sheet. Drop 1 tablespoonful of dark dough next to light dough with sides touching. Repeat with remaining dough, placing cookies 2 inches apart. Bake 7 to 9 minutes or until edges are lightly browned. Transfer cookies to a wire rack to cool. Store in an airtight container.

Yield: about 2 dozen cookies

FIG BARS

DOUGH
¹/₂ cup butter or margarine, softened
¹/₂ cup granulated sugar
¹/₂ cup firmly packed brown sugar
¹/₃ cup honey
1 egg
1 teaspoon vanilla extract
2¹/₄ cups all-purpose flour
1 cup whole-wheat flour
³/₄ teaspoon baking soda
¹/₂ teaspoon salt

FILLING
2 cups finely chopped dried figs (about 8 ounces)
1¹/₃ cups water
1 cup sugar
¹/₄ cup all-purpose flour
¹/₃ cup chopped walnuts
3 tablespoons orange juice

For dough, cream butter and sugars in large bowl until fluffy. Add honey, egg, an vanilla; beat until smooth. In a medium bowl, combine flours, baking soda, and salt. Add dry ingredients to creamed mixture; stir until a soft dough forms. Divide dough into fourths. Wrap in plastic wrap and chill 1 hour.

For filling, combine figs and water in a heavy medium saucepan over medium he Stirring constantly, bring mixture to a boi boil 5 minutes. In a small bowl, combine sugar and flour; stir into fig mixture. Reduce heat to medium-low. Stirring frequently, cook mixture 10 minutes or until thickened. Remove from heat. Stir ir walnuts and orange juice. Allow mixture t cool.

Preheat oven to 350 degrees. On a she of plastic wrap, use a floured rolling pin to roll out one fourth of dough into an 8 x 12-inch rectangle. Cut dough crosswi into four 3 x 8-inch pieces. Spread 2 tablespoons fig mixture down center of

ach length of dough. Slightly overlapping
dges, fold long sides of each dough strip
ver filling in center. Using plastic wrap to
ft dough, place dough strips, seam side
own, 2 inches apart on an ungreased
aking sheet. Bake 11 to 13 minutes or
ntil lightly browned. Cool cookies on pan
minutes; transfer to a wire rack to cool
ompletely. Cut into 2-inch-long bars.
epeat with remaining dough. Store in an
rtight container.

ield: about 5 dozen bars

RIDGE PARTNERS

    1 cup butter or margarine,
          softened
1/2 cups sifted confectioners sugar
    1 egg
    1 teaspoon vanilla extract
    2 cups all-purpose flour
 1/2 cup cocoa
 1/2 teaspoon salt

  In a large bowl, cream butter and
onfectioners sugar until fluffy. Add egg and
nilla; beat until smooth. In a small bowl,
ombine flour, cocoa, and salt. Add dry
gredients to creamed mixture; stir until a
ft dough forms. Divide dough in half.
rap in plastic wrap and chill 1 hour.
  Preheat oven to 375 degrees. On a lightly
oured surface, use a floured rolling pin to
oll out half of dough to 1/4-inch thickness.
se a 2 1/4 x 2 1/2-inch playing card suit-
aped cookie cutters to cut out cookies.
ransfer to an ungreased baking sheet.
ake 5 to 7 minutes or until bottoms are
ghtly browned. Transfer cookies to a wire
ack to cool. Repeat with remaining dough.
ore in an airtight container.

ield: about 4 dozen cookies

*Deal your bridge club a winning hand with these easy-to-make Bridge
Partners. A pretty basket filled with the chocolaty shortbread diamonds,
hearts, clubs, and spades is sure to be your trump card.*

GOODIES FOR GIVING

Nothing says "I love you" like a homemade gift, and when it includes something yummy from your oven, it's that much sweeter. You'll find an array of goodies for giving — whether you're looking for something to celebrate a birthday, express your thanks, or just brighten someone's day. And we've even shown you some pretty packaging ideas for making each delivery special! Whenever you want to let a loved one know how much you care, turn to this heartwarming collection.

Chocolate-Mint Surprises	Victorian Stamped Cookies
Walnut Crisps	Artist's Palette Cookies
Raspberry-Cream Cheese Brownies	Chocolate-Nut Sundae Squares
Heart Cookies	Doggie Treats

Sugared Chocolate Pretzels

(Previous page) *Walnut Crisps (from left) are light and crunchy fare that combine the flavors of walnuts and cinnamon. Heart Cookies get a burst of flavor from raspberry jelly. Wonderfully rich, Raspberry-Cream Cheese Brownies are extra-moist treats you'll want to reserve for those you truly adore! Chocolate-Mint Surprises have a minty center that's fresh and cool.*

CHOCOLATE-MINT SURPRISES

- 2/3 cup butter or margarine, softened
- 1 2/3 cups sugar
- 1/2 cup sour cream
- 1 egg
- 1 teaspoon vanilla extract
- 2 ounces unsweetened baking chocolate, melted
- 1 3/4 cups all-purpose flour
- 1/2 teaspoon baking powder
- 1/2 teaspoon baking soda
- 1/4 teaspoon salt
- 30 individually wrapped layered chocolate mints, halved (about 1/2 of a 10-ounce package)

Preheat oven to 375 degrees. In a large bowl, cream butter and sugar until fluffy. Add sour cream, egg, and vanilla; beat until smooth. Stir in melted chocolate. In a small bowl, combine flour, baking powder, baking soda, and salt. Add dry ingredients to creamed mixture; stir until a soft dough forms. Line a baking sheet with parchment paper. Drop a scant 1/2 tablespoon of dough onto prepared baking sheet, place half a mint on dough, and top with another scant 1/2 tablespoon dough. Repeat with remaining dough and mints, placing cookies 3 inches apart. Bake 9 to 11 minutes or until edges are crisp but centers are soft. Cool cookies on pan

2 minutes; transfer to a wire rack to cool completely. Store in an airtight container.

Yield: about 4 1/2 dozen cookies

WALNUT CRISPS

- 1/2 cup butter or margarine, softened
- 1/2 cup sugar
- 1 egg
- 1 teaspoon vanilla extract
- 1 1/4 cups all-purpose flour
- 1 teaspoon baking powder
- 1/2 teaspoon ground cinnamon
- 1 cup finely chopped walnuts
    Sugar

Preheat oven to 375 degrees. In a large bowl, cream butter and 1/2 cup sugar until fluffy. Add egg and vanilla; beat until smooth. In a small bowl, combine flour, baking powder, and cinnamon. Add dry ingredients to creamed mixture; stir until a soft dough forms. Stir in walnuts. Shape dough into 1-inch balls and roll in sugar. Place balls 2 inches apart on an ungreased baking sheet; flatten with bottom of a glass dipped in sugar. Bake 6 to 8 minutes or until edges are lightly browned. Transfer cookies to a wire rack to cool. Store in a cookie tin.

Yield: about 4 dozen cookies

RASPBERRY-CREAM CHEESE BROWNIES

TOPPING
- 11 ounces cream cheese, softened
- 1/3 cup sugar
- 1 egg
- 1 teaspoon vanilla extract

BROWNIES
- 1 cup butter or margarine, softened
- 1 2/3 cups sugar
- 3 eggs
- 6 ounces semisweet baking chocolate, melted
- 2 teaspoons vanilla extract

- 1 3/4 cups all-purpose flour
- 1/2 cup seedless raspberry jam

Preheat oven to 350 degrees. For topping, beat cream cheese and sugar in a medium bowl until smooth. Add egg and vanilla; beat until well blended. Set aside.

For brownies, beat butter and sugar in a large bowl until fluffy. Add eggs, 1 at a time, continuing to beat after each addition. Add melted chocolate, vanilla, and flour; stir until well blended. Spread chocolate mixture into 2 greased 8-inch square baking pans. Spread cream cheese mixture over chocolate mixture. Spoon jam over cream cheese mixture. Use a knife to swirl jam through cream cheese mixture. Bake 38 to 40 minutes or until center is almost set. Cool in pans. Cut into 1 1/2-inch squares. Store in an airtight container.

Yield: two 8-inch pans, about 25 brownies each

HEART COOKIES

- 3/4 cup butter or margarine, softened
- 1/2 cup sugar
- 1 egg
- 1 teaspoon almond extract
- 1/2 teaspoon vanilla extract
- 1 3/4 cups all-purpose flour
- 3 tablespoons cornstarch
- 1/2 teaspoon baking powder
- 1/8 teaspoon salt
- 1/3 cup raspberry jelly

Preheat oven to 350 degrees. In a medium bowl, cream butter and sugar until fluffy. Add egg and extracts; beat until smooth. In a small bowl, combine flour, cornstarch, baking powder, and salt. Add dry ingredients to creamed mixture; stir until a soft dough forms. On a lightly floured surface, use a floured rolling pin to roll out dough to 1/8-inch thickness. Use a 2 1/4-inch wide heart-shaped cookie cutter to cut out cookies. Transfer to a greased baking sheet

a ¾-inch-wide heart-shaped cookie
ter to cut out centers of half of cookies
baking sheet. Bake 10 to 12 minutes or
il edges are lightly browned. Transfer
okies to a wire rack to cool. Spread a
a layer of raspberry jelly on top of each
ole cookie and place a heart cutout
kie on top. Store in an airtight
tainer.

ld: about 2½ dozen cookies

CTORIAN STAMPED COOKIES

- ⁄4 cup butter or margarine, softened
- ⁄4 cup firmly packed brown sugar
- 1 egg
- 1 teaspoon vanilla extract
- ⁄2 teaspoon butter extract
- ⁄4 cups all-purpose flour
- ⁄8 teaspoon salt

n a large bowl, cream butter and brown
ar until fluffy. Add egg and extracts; beat
il smooth. In a medium bowl, combine
r and salt. Add dry ingredients to
amed mixture; stir until a soft dough
ms. Cover dough and chill 1 hour.
reheat oven to 350 degrees. Shape
gh into 1-inch balls and place 2 inches
rt on a greased baking sheet. Flatten
ls with a 2-inch-diameter cookie stamp
epared according to manufacturer's
ctions). Bake 9 to 11 minutes or until
toms are lightly browned. Transfer
kies to a wire rack to cool. Store in an
ight container.

ld: about 5 dozen cookies

*Lightly embossed with cookie stamps, our Victorian Stamped Cookies offer
an elegant way to say "thank you" to a dear friend.*

ARTIST'S PALETTE COOKIES

COOKIES

- 1 1/2 cups old-fashioned oats
- 1 cup butter or margarine, softened
- 1 1/4 cups sugar
- 2 eggs
- 1 teaspoon vanilla extract
- 2 1/4 cups all-purpose flour
- 1 teaspoon baking soda
- 1/2 teaspoon salt
- 3/4 cup chopped pecans, toasted and finely ground

ICING

- 2 cups sifted confectioners sugar
- 1/2 teaspoon vanilla extract
- 3 tablespoons plus 1 teaspoon milk

  Red, blue, green, and yellow liquid food coloring and 4 small-tipped squeeze bottles to decorate

Note: Use pattern, page 119, and follow Cutting Out Cookies, page 122.

For cookies, place oats in a food processor. Process until finely ground. In a large bowl, cream butter and sugar until fluffy. Add eggs and vanilla; beat until smooth. In a medium bowl, combine processed oats, flour, baking soda, and salt. Add dry ingredients to creamed mixture; stir until a soft dough forms. Stir in pecans. Divide dough in half. Wrap in plastic wrap and chill 1 hour.

Preheat oven to 350 degrees. On a lightly floured surface, use a floured rolling pin to roll out half of dough to 1/8-inch thickness. Cut out cookies. Place 1 inch apart on a greased baking sheet. Use the end of a drinking straw to cut holes in cookies. Bake 6 to 8 minutes or until edges are lightly browned. Transfer cookies to a wire rack to cool. Repeat with remaining dough.

For icing, combine confectioners sugar, vanilla, and milk in a medium bowl; stir until smooth. Place about 3 tablespoons

Surprise your creative friends with your own work of art — treat them to a showing of Artist's Palette Cookies. Simply use our pattern to create the "palettes" and then add splashes of colored icing for the "paint." They'll think the light pecan-flavored cookies are truly masterpieces!

icing in each of 4 small bowls and tint red, blue, green, and yellow. Spoon each color of icing into a separate squeeze bottle.

Decorate cookies with icing. Allow icing to harden. Store in an airtight container.

Yield: about 8 dozen cookies

A gaily decorated basket of Chocolate-Nut Sundae Squares makes a delightful birthday present! Chock-full of maraschino cherries and chopped pecans, the moist squares are topped with a drizzling of chocolate.

CHOCOLATE-NUT SUNDAE SQUARES

1/2 cup butter or margarine, softened
2/3 cup firmly packed brown sugar
1 egg
1 jar (10 ounces) maraschino
 cherries, drained and chopped,
 reserving 1/4 cup liquid
1/2 teaspoon vanilla extract
1/2 cups all-purpose flour
1/2 cup chocolate mix for milk
1/2 teaspoon baking powder
1 cup chopped pecans

1/3 cup semisweet chocolate chips
1/2 teaspoon vegetable shortening

Preheat oven to 350 degrees. In a large bowl, cream butter and brown sugar until fluffy. Add egg, reserved cherry liquid, and vanilla; beat until smooth. In a small bowl, combine flour, chocolate mix, and baking powder. Add dry ingredients to creamed mixture; stir until a soft dough forms. Stir in pecans and cherries. Line a 9-inch square baking pan with aluminum foil, extending foil over opposite sides of pan; grease foil. Spread mixture into prepared pan. Bake 20 to 25 minutes or until firm. Cool in pan 10 minutes. Lift from pan using ends of foil. Cool completely. Melt chocolate chips and shortening in a small saucepan over low heat. Drizzle melted chocolate over baked mixture. Cut into 2-inch squares. Store in an airtight container.

Yield: about 16 squares

If your gift list includes a four-legged pal, then rustle up a batch of bone-shaped Doggie Treats. The crispy cookies are baked with whole wheat flour and Cheddar cheese for hearty goodness. They also make a nice gift for a friend with a new pet when delivered in a food dish decorated with a leash "bow."

DOGGIE TREATS

1¼ cups finely shredded Cheddar
    cheese
½ cup vegetable oil
¼ cup beef or chicken broth
2 cloves garlic, minced
1 cup whole-wheat flour
½ cup all-purpose flour
½ cup cornmeal
¼ cup nonfat dry milk powder

Preheat oven to 300 degrees. In a large bowl, combine cheese, oil, broth, and garlic. In a small bowl, combine flours, cornmeal, and dry milk. Gradually stir dry ingredients into cheese mixture; stir or knead until well blended.

On a lightly floured surface, use a floured rolling pin to roll out dough to ¼-inch thickness. Use a 2½-inch-long bone-shaped cookie cutter to cut out treats. Transfer to a greased baking sheet. Bake 24 to 26 minutes or until firm and bottoms are lightly browned. Transfer treats to a wire rack to cool. Store in an airtight container in a cool place.

Yield: about 5 dozen dog treats

SUGARED CHOCOLATE PRETZELS

3/4 cup butter or margarine, softened
2/3 cup granulated sugar
1 egg
1 tablespoon honey
1/2 teaspoons vanilla extract
2 cups all-purpose flour
1/3 cup cocoa
1/2 teaspoons baking powder
1/4 teaspoon salt
Coarse white decorating sugar

In a large bowl, cream butter and granulated sugar until fluffy. Add egg, honey, and vanilla; beat until smooth. In a small bowl, combine flour, cocoa, baking powder, and salt. Add dry ingredients to creamed mixture; stir until a soft dough forms. Divide dough into fourths. Wrap in plastic wrap and chill 1 hour.

Preheat oven to 350 degrees. Working with one fourth of dough, divide into pieces. Roll each piece of dough into a inch-long rope. Roll in decorating sugar. Twist 2 ropes of dough together. Place on a greased baking sheet. Repeat with remaining ropes. Bake 9 to 11 minutes or until edges are slightly firm and bottoms are browned. Cool pretzels on pan 2 minutes; transfer to a wire rack to cool completely. Repeat with remaining dough. Store in an airtight container.

Yield: 2 dozen pretzels

Here's a new twist on an old favorite — our Sugared Chocolate Pretzels are made with cocoa and a touch of honey and then rolled in sugar before baking! For a sunny presentation, wrap the braided treats in cellophane and tuck them in a pot of silk sunflowers. They're sure to brighten a loved one's day!

PATTERNS

NEW YEAR'S TOAST COOKIES

(Page 13)

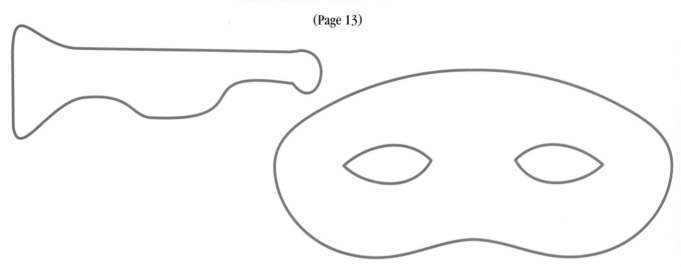

CHOCOLATE-PEANUT BUTTER COOKIES

(Page 15)

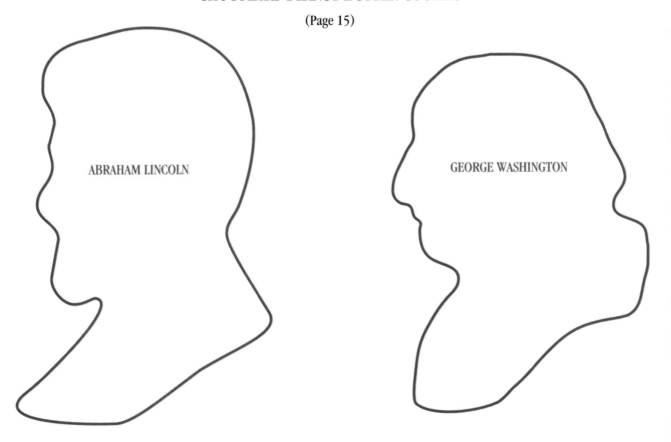

ABRAHAM LINCOLN

GEORGE WASHINGTON

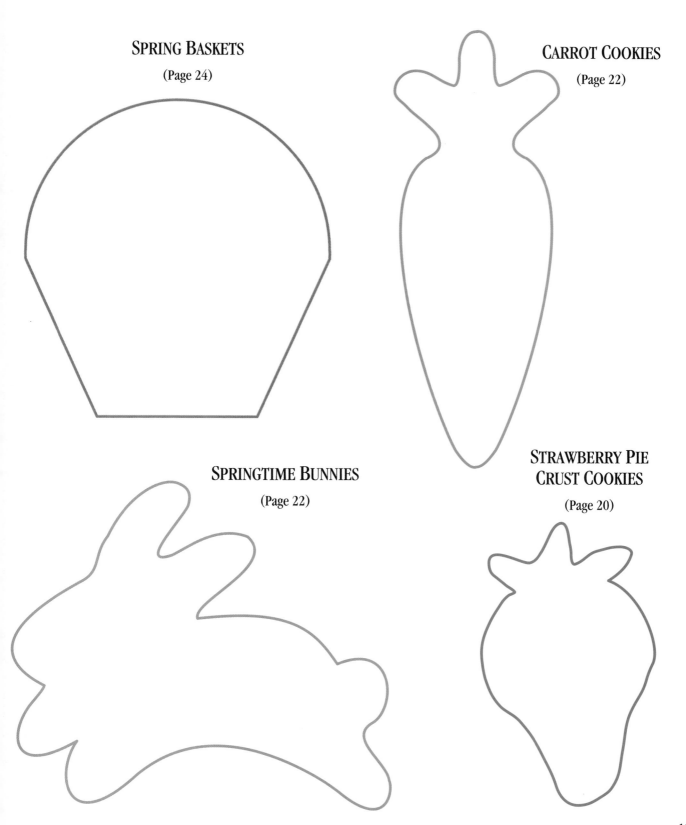

SPRING BASKETS

(Page 24)

CARROT COOKIES

(Page 22)

SPRINGTIME BUNNIES

(Page 22)

STRAWBERRY PIE
CRUST COOKIES

(Page 20)

PATTERNS (continued)

SWEET HEARTS

(Page 96)

ROOT BEER FLOATS

(Page 64)

SPICED CHRISTMAS STARS

(Page 49)

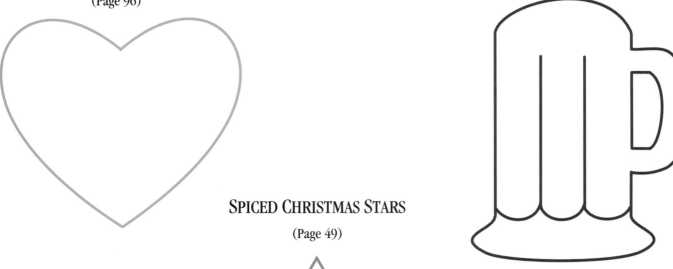

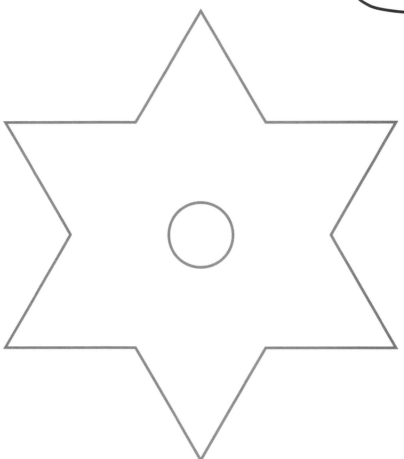

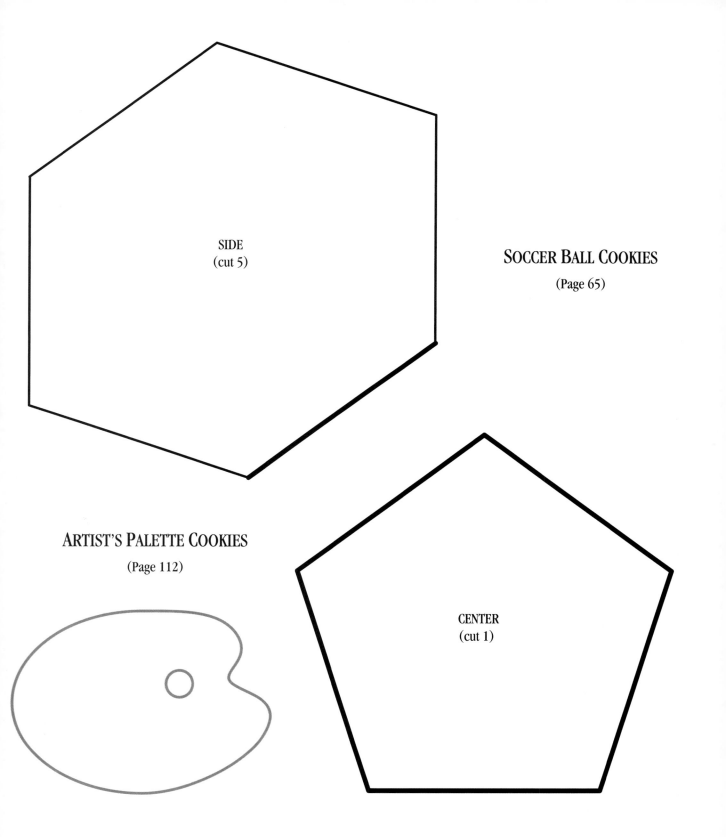

SIDE
(cut 5)

SOCCER BALL COOKIES

(Page 65)

ARTIST'S PALETTE COOKIES

(Page 112)

CENTER
(cut 1)

ALMOND COOKIE TREE

(Page 72)

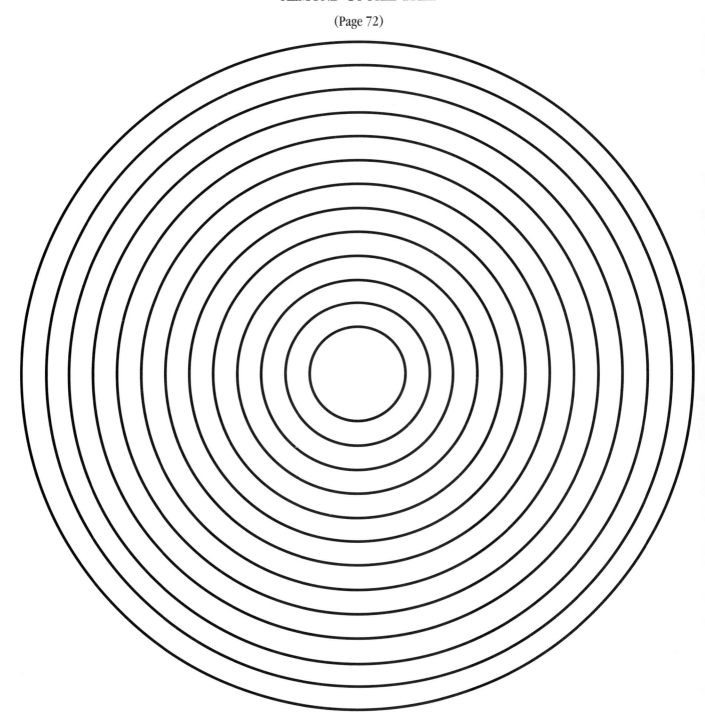

KITCHEN TIPS

MEASURING INGREDIENTS

Liquid measuring cups have a rim above the measuring line to keep liquid ingredients from spilling. Nested measuring cups are used to measure dry ingredients, butter, shortening, and peanut butter. Measuring spoons are used for measuring both dry and liquid ingredients.

To measure flour or granulated sugar: Spoon ingredient into nested measuring cup and level off with a knife. Do not pack down with spoon.

To measure confectioners sugar: Sift sugar, spoon lightly into nested measuring cup, and level off with a knife.

To measure brown sugar: Pack sugar into nested measuring cup and level off with a knife. Sugar should hold its shape when removed from cup.

To measure dry ingredients equaling less than 1/4 cup: Dip measuring spoon into ingredient and level off with a knife.

To measure butter, shortening, or peanut butter: Pack ingredient firmly into nested measuring cup and level off with a knife.

To measure liquids: Use a liquid measuring cup placed on a flat surface. Pour ingredient into cup and check measuring line at eye level.

To measure honey or syrup: For a more accurate measurement, lightly spray measuring cup or spoon with cooking spray before measuring so the liquid will release easily from cup or spoon.

SOFTENING BUTTER OR MARGARINE

To soften butter, remove wrapper from butter and place on a microwave-safe plate. Microwave 1 stick 20 to 30 seconds at medium-low power (30%).

SOFTENING CREAM CHEESE

To soften cream cheese, remove wrapper from cream cheese and place on a microwave-safe plate. Microwave 1 to 1 1/2 minutes at medium power (50%) for an 8-ounce package or 30 to 45 seconds for a 3-ounce package.

WHIPPING CREAM

For greatest volume, chill a glass bowl, beaters, and cream until well chilled before whipping. In warm weather, place chilled bowl over ice while whipping cream.

TOASTING NUTS

To toast nuts, spread nuts on an ungreased baking sheet. Stirring occasionally, bake 8 to 10 minutes in a preheated 350-degree oven or until nuts are slightly darker in color.

PREPARING CITRUS FRUIT ZEST

To remove outer portion of peel (colored part) from citrus fruits, use a fine grater or fruit zester, being careful not to cut into the bitter white portion. Zest is also referred to as grated peel.

BEATING EGG WHITES

For greatest volume, beat egg whites at room temperature in a clean, dry metal or glass bowl.

TO BLANCH ALMONDS

Place 1 cup water in a 1-quart bowl or casserole; cover. Microwave on high power (100%) 3 minutes. Add 1 cup whole shelled almonds. Microwave on high power (100%) 1 minute uncovered; drain and remove peel from nuts. Dry on paper towels.

USING CHOCOLATE

Chocolate is best stored in a cool, dry place. Since it has a high content of cocoa butter, chocolate may develop a grey film, or "bloom," when temperatures change. This grey film does not affect the taste.

When melting chocolate, a low temperature is important to prevent overheating and scorching that will affect flavor and texture. The following are methods for melting chocolate:

Chocolate can be melted in a heavy saucepan over low heat, stirring constantly until melted.

Melting chocolate in a double boiler over hot, not boiling, water is a good method to prevent chocolate from overheating.

Using a microwave to melt chocolate is fast and convenient. To microwave chocolate, place in a microwave-safe container and cook on medium-high power (80%) 1 minute; stir with a dry spoon. Continue to microwave 15 seconds at a time, stirring chocolate after each interval until smooth. Frequent stirring is important, as the chocolate will appear not to be melting, but will be soft when stirred. A shiny appearance is another sign that chocolate is melting.

COOKIE TIPS

CUTTING OUT COOKIES

Place a piece of white paper over pattern (for a more durable pattern, use acetate, a thin plastic used for stenciling that is available at craft stores). Use a permanent felt-tip pen with fine point to trace pattern; cut out pattern. Place pattern on rolled-out dough and use a small sharp knife to cut out cookies. (*Note:* If dough is sticky, frequently dip knife into flour while cutting out cookies.)

CUTTING DIAMOND-SHAPED BARS

To cut 1 3/4-inch-wide x 3-inch-long diamond-shaped pieces, start at 1 short edge of pan and make 1 1/2-inch-wide cuts (Fig. 1).

Fig. 1

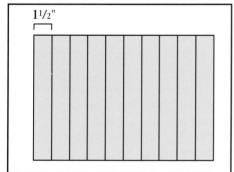

Make a diagonal cut from lower left corner to upper right corner (shown by heavy black line). Make 1 1/2 inch-wide cuts on each side of first diagonal cut (Fig. 2).

Fig. 2

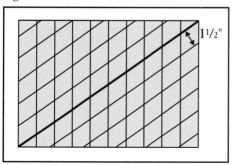

BAKING TIPS

Chilling dough: To speed up chilling of dough, place in freezer about 20 minutes for each hour of chilling time indicated in recipe. If dough is to be rolled out into a rectangle or circle, shaping it into that form before chilling will make rolling out the dough much easier.

Eggs: Recipes were tested using large eggs.

Butter: Recipes were tested using salted butter, unless otherwise specified in recipe. When softening butter in the microwave, be careful not to let it melt, as melted butter results in a flatter cookie. If margarine is used, use one labeled "margarine" instead of "spread." Corn oil margarines will make a softer dough, which will increase chilling time.

Dutch Process Cocoa: A richer, darker cocoa, Dutch process cocoa is available in the baking section of most supermarkets and is a refined cocoa that has a more mellow flavor. Regular cocoa can be substituted, but the flavor will be slightly different.

Greasing baking sheets and pans: Use a thin coating of vegetable shortening to grease baking sheets. When lowfat recipes were tested, pans were sprayed with vegetable cooking spray.

Cooling baking sheets: Cool baking sheets between batches so cookies will keep their shape.

Baking batches of cookies: Bake one batch of cookies at a time on the center rack of a preheated oven. If baking two batches at a time, space racks evenly in oven. Allow 1 to 2 inches of space around baking sheet for good air circulation.

Testing for doneness: Use recipe instructions to test for doneness. Since oven temperatures may vary, always check cookies 1 minute before the earliest time stated in recipe to prevent overbaking.

Cooling cookies: Immediately remove cookies from pan unless otherwise stated recipe. Use a spatula to transfer cookies to wire rack. If cookies cool and stick to pan return pan to a warm oven for a few minutes to allow cookies to soften.

Lining pans: When recipe says to line a pan with foil or waxed paper, grease pan first to help keep foil or waxed paper in place. Then grease foil or waxed paper if stated in recipe.

Using cookie cutters: To keep dough from sticking to cookie cutters, dip in flour before cutting out each cookie.

Using a plastic bag to decorate: When you need to drizzle a small amount of icing or melted chocolate and you do not have a pastry bag, use a resealable plastic bag. After filling bag half full of icing or chocolate, seal the bag and cut off a small tip of one corner. Make your first snip small, as you can always cut off more if needed.

Spacing cookies on baking sheet: Leave enough space between cookies to allow them to spread. Most recipes will give you the number of inches.

SUPPLIES

Cookie cutters: A good cutting edge, usually found on metal cookie cutters, makes a clean edge on cookies. Plastic cutters do not always cut as well as metal. Cookie cutters used in these recipes were either measured from inside edges across the widest part or the width was given and then the height. To prevent metal cookie cutters from rusting, wash, wipe dry, and place in a warm oven to dry thoroughly before storing.

Spoons and scoops: Unless otherwise specified in recipe, use a tableware teaspoon or tablespoon for drop cookies. Cookie scoops are available in different sizes and are easy to use. They produce uniformly sized cookies that will bake more evenly.

Baking sheets: Use heavy-gauge, shiny aluminum sheets with low or no sides for even browning of cookies. Nonstick cookie sheets produce cookies that spread less and have smoother bottoms, but their dark coating will affect browning.

Insulated cookie sheets will help prevent overbaking of cookies, but bottoms will not brown, making it difficult to determine doneness in some cookies. If bottoms do brown, cookies may be overdone. Also, cookies with a high butter content will spread out before the shape is set, so edges may be thin. Baking time will be slightly longer on insulated sheets. Cookies were not tested using insulated sheets, so times will need to be adjusted.

Jellyroll pan: Use a metal pan with at least 1-inch sides to prevent batter from overflowing. A standard size pan is $10\frac{1}{2}$ x $15\frac{1}{2}$ x 1 inch.

Parchment paper: This paper is available in kitchen specialty stores or in cake decorating sections of craft or department stores. Using parchment paper eliminates the need to grease cookie sheets and makes cleanup easy. Some recipes specify using parchment paper; when cookies were tested, it was necessary to use parchment paper to prevent sticking.

Electric mixer: All recipes were tested using a hand-held mixer. When recipes state to cream or beat ingredients, a mixer was used. However, they can also be mixed by hand.

Timer: Baking times for cookies are usually short, and a few extra minutes may result in an unsatisfactory product. Use a timer to ensure accuracy. It is also helpful to have a timer that has a continuous signal instead of one that gives one short signal.

Ruler: A ruler will give accurate results for measuring the thickness to slice rolled cookie dough, the distance between cookies on baking sheet, the thickness of rolled-out dough, and cutting bar cookies.

Cookie press: This is a tube-shaped tool used to make decorative cookies. The press comes with several discs that create different cookie shapes when the dough is pressed through them. This is a fast method of producing uniformly sized cookies.

Wire cooling racks: These racks allow air to circulate around cookies as they cool, preventing soggy cookies. Place cookies in a single layer on racks. Unless otherwise specified in recipe, cool bar cookies in the pan on a wire rack.

Pastry bags: These bags are also called decorating bags and are available in soft canvas with a plastic lining, reusable plastic, disposable plastic, and parchment paper. When fitted with decorating tips, they are used to form decorative designs or to control the amount of icing or glaze drizzled on cookies. Some cookies are formed by squeezing dough through a large tip attached to a pastry bag.

Rolling pin: A long, heavy rolling pin works well with cookies. Covering the rolling pin with a stockinette cover (available with kitchen specialty items) helps keep the dough from sticking.

STORAGE TIPS

• Cookies should be completely cooled before storing.

• Store each kind of cookie separately to prevent flavors from blending. Soft cookies will cause crisp cookies to become soft.

• Store soft cookies in an airtight container. Use waxed paper between layers to prevent cookies from sticking together.

• Store crisp cookies in a tin or container with a loose-fitting lid. In humid areas, the lid will need to be tighter so cookies will stay crisp.

• Store bar cookies in the pan covered with foil or remove from pan and store in an airtight container.

• If soft cookies have dried out, place a slice of apple or bread with cookies for a few days in an airtight container.

• Most cookies (except meringues) can be frozen up to six months. Freeze in plastic freezer bags or plastic containers with tight-fitting lids. Freeze iced cookies between layers of waxed paper after icing has hardened, or wait and ice cookies when thawed and ready to eat. To serve, unwrap and allow cookies to thaw 15 minutes.

• Wrapping cookies in clear cellophane makes a nice way to present them as a gift.

MAILING TIPS

Soft, moist cookies and bar cookies are suitable for mailing. Line a sturdy box with waxed paper, aluminum foil, or plastic wrap. Place a layer of crumpled waxed paper or paper towels in bottom of box. Depending on type of cookie, wrap back-to-back if they are flat, in small groups in plastic bags, or individually.

Pack crumpled waxed paper or paper towels snugly between cookies to prevent them from shifting. Tape box securely closed.

EQUIVALENT MEASUREMENTS

1 tablespoon	=	3 teaspoons
$1/8$ cup (1 fluid ounce)	=	2 tablespoons
$1/4$ cup (2 fluid ounces)	=	4 tablespoons
$1/3$ cup	=	$5 1/3$ tablespoons
$1/2$ cup (4 fluid ounces)	=	8 tablespoons
$3/4$ cup (6 fluid ounces)	=	12 tablespoons
1 cup (8 fluid ounces)	=	16 tablespoons or $1/2$ pint
2 cups (16 fluid ounces)	=	1 pint
1 quart (32 fluid ounces)	=	2 pints
$1/2$ gallon (64 fluid ounces)	=	2 quarts
1 gallon (128 fluid ounces)	=	4 quarts

HELPFUL FOOD EQUIVALENTS OR SUBSTITUTIONS

$1/2$ cup butter	=	1 stick butter
1 square baking chocolate	=	1 ounce chocolate
1 cup chocolate chips	=	6 ounces chocolate chips
$2 1/4$ cups packed brown sugar	=	1 pound brown sugar
$3 1/2$ cups unsifted confectioners sugar	=	1 pound confectioners sugar
2 cups granulated sugar	=	1 pound granulated sugar
4 cups all-purpose flour	=	1 pound all-purpose flour
2 tablespoons grated orange zest	=	1 medium orange
4 cups chopped pecans or walnuts	=	1 pound shelled pecans or walnuts
1 ounce unsweetened chocolate	=	3 tablespoons cocoa plus 1 tablespoon vegetable shortening
1 teaspoon baking powder	=	$1/2$ teaspoon cream of tartar plus $1/4$ teaspoon baking soda
1 container (4 ounces) whole candied cherries	=	5 ounces chopped cherries

RECIPE INDEX

CREDITS

To the talented people who helped in the creation of the following recipes in this book, we extend a special word of thanks:

- *Poppy Seed Cookies,* page 12: Merrell C. Mastin
- *Chocolate Crinkle Cookies,* page 41: Jacqueline Krebs
- *Chewy Fruitcake Bars,* page 48: Genevieve Maxwell
- *Old-fashioned Gingersnaps,* page 58: Helen Goodwin
- *Oatmeal Family Favorites,* page 59: Sue Butler
- *Cashew Dreams,* page 70: Nora Faye Spencer Clift
- *Turkish Almond Cookies,* page 86: Guniz Cakmak
- *Trail Cookies,* page 104: Marilyn Mastny

We want to extend a warm *thank you* to the generous people who allowed us to use their antique cookie jars in our photographs: Lee Kipp, Elaine Wolff, Susan Johnson, and Kay Smart.

A very special *thank you* goes to Dr. and Mrs. Michael Grounds for the unlimited use of their cookie jar collection.

We also want to thank Shirley Held for allowing us to photograph our *Sophisticated Tastes* collection in her home.

To Magna IV Color Imaging of Little Rock, Arkansas, we say thank you for the superb color reproduction and excellent pre-press preparation.

We especially want to thank photographer Larry Pennington of Peerless Photography, Little Rock, Arkansas, for his time, patience, and excellent work.